Growing Your
Own Truth

Growing Your Own Truth

A Guide To Coming Out As Gay

Andrew Phineas

Library of Congress Control Number:		2020912922
ISBN:	Hardcover	978-1-7960-5513-9
	Softcover	978-1-7960-5512-2
	eBook	978-1-7960-5511-5

Print information available on the last page.

Rev. date: 07/17/2020

To order additional copies of this book, contact:
Xlibris
1-888-795-4274
www.Xlibris.com
Orders@Xlibris.com
798590

CONTENTS

Dedicated to my wonderful gay big brother, Matt and to the man of my dreams, whom I finally found, Luis Guerra.

And after and for a long time to come he'd have reason to evoke the recollection of those smiles and to reflect upon the good will which provoked them for it had power to heal men and to bring them to safety long after all other resources were exhausted.

—Cormac McCarthy

Most names of actual people and places have been changed in this account to protect the privacy of others.

CHAPTER 1

The Philosophical Landscape

The Meaning of Truth

I grew up in a family, tradition, and religious community that thinks of truth only as an objective, unchanging, and immutable thing, so I found it strange when I first heard a reference to one's own truth. I didn't understand how a person could have a different truth from others while the belief is still true, but in my process of coming out as a gay man, I learned to respect the reality of my feelings and experience, my own truth, and the truth of others, while being my own person, separate from the beliefs espoused by others. This is my very personal story of coming out as gay and learning how truth grows inside us as we tend its garden rather than coming fully formed from outside, like canned vegetables from the grocery store. I'm not sure if this is primarily a book of philosophy or a personal narrative, but I hope it can be both, and I hope it can help others through difficult processes of transition to clarify and validate the existence of private truth for those who, like me, used to understand truth only in a more exclusive sense. The philosophy and a tell-all narrative fit well together because they help illustrate one another, and that is how I have written this book.

I came out as gay almost five years ago, and now I'm working out the details to marry my same-sex partner and to evaluate the truth I think I've found. The journey and the ups and downs led me to wonder how I got to this point in my life, how and why this change had taken place, and to evaluate my progress and my future. Most of all, how have I come to feel good about a life so different from the one I was living previously and so different from the values of mainstream culture? Have I just simply lost my mind, and can my way of life really be called truth? Lots of food for thought, and I believe it is entertaining and instructive enough to share. In fact, one of the best things about personal truth is to share it with others and to encourage the truth of others to come out as well. My journey now seems to have come to an end with a wonderful partner, who is fun, loving, handsome, kind, and extremely interesting. But this end result seemed far from a given during the journey, and this book is about the journey rather than the end result or what I believe to be true.

Some events in this book have been relatively recent, and this is not a book on how to find a gay partner but is the story of my journey, learning truth through experience, and reflection. One of the deep discoveries of this journey was to come to peace with an unknown future. My future is now clearer, but I set this peace aside in order to relate to the reader and to give context to my discoveries along the way. The reader can share my journey but cannot share my boyfriend nor can I promise anything for the future of the reader, but I hope these reflections will bring peace to others on their independent journeys.

Truth is a belief that when one takes it as an assumption, it proves to be a reliable guide and predictor for the unknown. This is my truth and the narrative details how it guided me. This guide may not work for everyone, but I offer it for those who may be in need of an atypical model.

The Limited Truth of Conformity

I believe in absolute Truth as revealed by and embodied by the Divine, but my personal life and the pages of history show far too much abuse of individual perspectives by a Truth wielded by the majority. I plan to speak for the delicate spark inside each of us not as a substitute for the Divine but as an interconnected manifestation of it. Personal truth is not to be hidden away and kept personal but shared and related to others as each of us listen and try to understand the truths of others, which I believe may make a beautiful and complete perspective together. I do not have the answer, but I want to provoke the reader with new perspectives through sharing my truth and hopefully fan the flames of truth inside each reader.

Strictly speaking, I don't think this can be a philosophy book because I'm not going to refer to or critique philosophers who have come before me or tell you that my way is correct. I will instead be emphasizing the truth that I found in me as an example of what each reader may find inside himself or herself, not an insistence that I have the Truth but perhaps something unique and new and different to inspire others to think more deeply. I want to downplay the dominance of, but not overthrow, absolute Truth to give space for the experience of each individual. Those who believe or have experience with the belief that Truth (note the capital letter) is absolute and all-powerful know the need for this breathing room. American politics offers a good example as we continue to believe that certain truths are self-evident and that America is the "greatest nation on earth" or, in the realm of religion, that receives truth from holy writ or long tradition. These ideas are believed to be inarguable because of the depth and length of time they have been believed. There is some sense to the notion that ideas that have lasted over time are more reliable than the truth of one person. However, that does not negate the availability of new perspectives, and if we give ourselves completely to absolute Truth, it is too easy to dismiss anything else, including the individual. I once heard a clergyman say that "if anyone preaches something new to you, that means it's probably wrong." It's comforting to believe in something that has always been true, and the sense of permanence is comforting in an uncertain world. But we are well served to learn confidence in our own perspectives and that of other individuals as well.

Family and societal expectations function this way too. Norms are quietly accepted because they have always been that way. For example, it was always assumed that children in my extended family would attend college or some kind of postsecondary education. It was expected of me, without direct discussion, and I expected it from my two daughters, although I don't remember ever telling them so. Somehow they got the message. One has a degree, and the younger is on her way. In the same way, there are certain expectations of attracting, coupling, and dating in societies that are unconsciously transmitted to all members of the group. For example, somehow I learned that I should feel inadequate when I didn't have a date for a school dance. When I went to those dances with male friends who were also vaguely inadequate, I learned from watching others how I was supposed to ask females to dance, that there were certain places where I was never supposed to put my hands on women, and I absorbed the "truth" that dancing with other boys was clearly out of bounds. So as I developed feelings for boys, I generally put those thoughts safely into the boxes already available to me. These kinds of truth are not thrust upon us by government conspiracy or a cabal of secretive priests but unconsciously created by each society. However, they can greatly misdirect, harm, and confuse the individual.

For me, I started my journey tripping over the ideals expected of me. Sometime in college, I defined my feelings for other men as the need to have one or more close male friends. I enjoyed these nonsexual friendships, and they became an essential part of my life. I even derived a sense of identity with one of my closest friends in that we were expected by the larger group to be together, almost like a couple. As I got older, I noticed that my interest in getting to know new friends was directly correlated to how physically attractive I found the men. So I called myself superficial because that designation was allowable, if undesirable, within the context of my society. However, just because an idea is widely believed does not make it true any more than if most people, like a piece of art, does that makes it the best. Each person knows his or her own needs and own mind and can best judge how a truth speaks or does not speak to him or her.

Truth should be in the business of connection, not coercion. It is this individual perspective I hope to encourage and nurture, not to praise those who believe like me or to smash the truth of others with a larger absolute Truth. But once cultivated to encourage us to share our truth, as I will do with you, to help broaden the understanding of Truth in ourselves and those around us as we share and understand one another, we learn and are inspired by one another.

CHAPTER 2

Not in Kansas Anymore

Defining Gravity

Here my journey begins. I found eventually that the generally held views on coupling did not match my thoughts, and a few of my desires went quite beyond the generally acceptable and needed places to roam. I found nude male figures in art much more attractive than the female figures, and in my early twenties, I had what could only be described as a series of crushes on men in my environment. I remember a cashier at the local grocery store with whom I was totally smitten. When he returned my change, I longed for him to touch my hand. Such out-of-bounds fantasies were disturbing because they didn't have a box to fit into, but I felt no requirement to label them or need to separate from the group because of them. I even told the woman I was engaged to at the time, whom I later married. She was not overly alarmed by my lust that gave "checkout line" a very seductive meaning, so I wasn't concerned either, and I got back to the life I was supposed to be living. After we were married for several years, I experienced sex with another man for the first time during a business trip, really enjoyed it, and tried to find opportunities to experience more. Unfortunately, I never saw the grocery clerk naked, nor did I really understand how to address the need or even understand the mechanics of gay love or sex. I think in *Star Trek*, they call that "moving on impulse power." For me, my needs and desires were true because they were my genuine feelings, but I had to keep them secret because society had no place in which to understand or accept these interests or behaviors, and if asked, I couldn't explain them either.

I would say that this was the beginning of my own truth. It began with respect for myself and what I knew about myself, what I needed and desired. I knew what I wanted and awkwardly pursued it despite society's lack of acceptance or even my own understanding of what was happening. These are the three primary criteria to the concept of one's own truth: first, it's strongly based in what the individual wants, needs, and believes; second, it's true from the individual's perspective; and third, it's separate and different from the generally accepted truth. I'm starting to also believe it's also essentially intuitive rather than reasoned, but that would be a discussion for a different and decidedly philosophical book. I tried to find a way to change my desires to conform with society and saw a string of religious and secular counselors. Many could not even understand what I was asking and instead spent time on peripheral issues that they felt more comfortable in handling, like loneliness. However, truth is not found in joining the right group and conforming. Our most valuable truth in ordering our lives comes from ourselves.

Our own truth starts out simply as ideas and beliefs that don't fit neatly into boxes and paradigms provided by the larger culture. It can also be new combinations of externally acceptable truth that we have put together in a different combination. As a child, when I began to imagine choosing a career, I found several combinations of activities I liked that could have been reasonable careers, and in the end, the career I chose was a combination of activities that I still liked over time. That was another facet of my truth. Some career ideas were appealing but didn't make the final cut. For example, my brief flirtation with becoming a doctor died in a difficult high school math class. So my experience helped define the truth of what would make a good career for me, and eventually, circumstances and new information caused me to steer closer to one career than another. I learned new things about myself and changed my course accordingly. The things I saw in my own desires and sexuality followed the same pattern but, by their nature, were held more in secret than career ideas that I felt free to discuss with all. These guideposts should be called truth because they are consistently true in my life experience.

Traditionalists would argue that one person's feelings are inferior and irrelevant because they do not reflect a larger and more generalizable Truth, Traditionally, Truth is only something that applies to everyone, but this is a very limited view of truth with little utility. For example, my career choice did not affect the larger moral picture, but it did direct much of my future life, so I would say it had more influence on me than the Ten Commandments, which deal with important but rare circumstances. Furthermore, specific moral truth is pointless to an individual if it does not fit his or her understanding of the world and specific questions. For example, how does a vegan interpret "Thou shalt not covet thy neighbor's cow"? A vegan has no use for a cow and so would have little desire to own one. There needs to be some rethinking and reapplication in order for the moral instruction to have any value. In the end, larger truths are evaluated and adopted or rejected by the individual.

Some thinkers take refuge at this point and search for definitions to include a multitude of personal experiences. I briefly toyed with the thought that perhaps I was a gay man who happened to be married to a woman. That seemed like nonsense to me, so I didn't pursue the thought further. In the same spirit, I've heard twenty-year-olds go to great lengths to describe exactly which kind of bisexual they are, and I've heard gays say that the whole idea of bisexuality is only a ruse for those who don't want to admit they are gay. Of course there's the traditional male dodge in the opposite direction, "Just because I had sex with a man doesn't mean I'm gay" or defining homosexuality or lack of it by the role one takes during a homosexual act. Unless you're a disciple of Aristotle, a definition does not lead to truth (disparaging a dead philosopher: check). My own initiatives, impulses and ideas seem more reliable guides to truth than external thinking and discussion.

CHAPTER 3

Managing Personal Truth

Personal truth helps to color and direct the choices of the individual who holds it, along with general principles that may be believed by a larger group, but again interpreted and applied by the individual. This individual spark is the essence of self, but as we will see later, individuals can learn a lot from others as they explain and listen to each other's truths together. That is friendship and relationship. If we are on individual journeys, the way to connection, then, is to offer something of self to connect and relate to others.

As I move through the world and meet new people, I have different levels of self-disclosure with different people depending on the goal of the interaction. I have recently moved to a new office at work, and self-revelation takes many forms. I have decided to be open with all officemates that I am gay. One colleague likes to hear my stories about introducing my boyfriend to American traditions and some of the joys and stresses of a new relationship. This colleague has become a friend as we talk about many life experiences besides my gayness. There are some male friends in the office with whom I carefully measure out my gay content or sometimes test their limits. I push their limits partly to be myself, and they do the same with me, sharing stories about their dog or truck or love of baseball, which I do not share. I have other friends with whom I go deeper to discuss big life lessons or share sad events or with whom I share my joy. Some of the office relationships may develop this depth over time, but for now we are still colleagues. I do flirt with some men as well, but that is a different set of behaviors. There are a few people, mostly family or very good friends, with whom I can spill the guts of my truth. As we build relationships, we chose what and how much to disclose about ourselves

Definitions Are Not the Self

However, it's important to remember that this personal truth itself, not a definition or a category are the true measure of self. An obsession with definitions leads people too often to speak of coming out as a one-time event, like joining a club or a religious conversion or maybe a single death-defying feat. There are some elements that feel this way to the individual coming out or perhaps to the people in his or her circle of friends and family as one applies a definition of self that separates the self from those who are listening or links the self with a group not present in the discussion. The use of a mutually understood definition makes the event quick, but there are some definite downsides to this kind of drive-by coming out, such as, "What does it mean to be gay?" Definitions vary widely. Are there certain talents that go with the title, like a heightened fashion sense? Or are certain preferences implied? Will the person who just came out suddenly have more interest in the musical theater or shoes or John Wayne movies? Are there implications for the person's political or religious beliefs? With new friends, I never say a sentence like "I am gay" because it leads to too much misunderstanding. I will usually lead with something else that implies the same content, like referring to my boyfriend is usually a safe start.

Second, the listener usually understands the magnitude of the statement and so wants to understand why the individual is making this statement and taking this step. Of course, before asking, most listeners spend a good deal of time making up their own assumed reasons for it. After I came out and explained that my worldview had changed, I found friends' and family members' made-up and assumed reasons quite entertaining. My father in particular spent months trying to imagine a reason before he finally broke down and asked me why I had come out. Does the new definition mean changes in personal relationships? Are more or certain types of sex required to be gay? A simple definition does not answer these potentially very important questions. So imagine a son comes home from college who says, "Dad, I'm gay." Dad is immediately trying to interpret what this means. Typical misperceptions that may arise in such an instance are to interpret it as "The child thinks I am a poor example of a man and a father and doesn't want to be like me." Or Dad thinks of the one gay man he knows and interprets that the son wants to be exactly like him, although many of that man's traits may have little to do with homosexuality. Definitions serve only to confuse and misdirect the user. Many young people are unsure about their sexual orientation, and from my experience, I have to say older people can wrestle with that problem as well. If the explorer thinks that to be gay means a particular set of norms and behaviors, he or she may peremptorily choose for or against the behaviors assumed to be required, depending on what he or she believes it to include. Exterior definitions do not matter as much as the inherent and inescapable attraction to the same sex. Each individual will construct his or her life from there. Knowing the self is important; finding the correct definition is not. So the importance of growing your own truth is key rather than finding the correct definition or acceptance by the right people.

People need to stop genuflecting to the known truth or assumptions of truth in their lives and step forward to do or believe what they feel. It was an important moment for me, as I came out as gay to myself when in this period of transition and confusion, I thought about prayer to ask for divine guidance and assistance. My first thought must have been picked up off someone else's garbage heap: "God doesn't love or want to hear from gay people." I hadn't yet worked out the theology, but my gut told me that initial thought was wrong and I threw out that flea-infested idea, believing instead that man was created to praise God, which yes, I had heard somewhere and accepted as my own. Therefore, just as being gay did not disqualify me from being human, why would it disqualify me from praising or pleasing God? I later found pieces of received truth in scripture, which support this response, but for that pivotal moment. I praised God on my way to a gay date, based on what I felt to be true and afterward even more so because the guy was a great kisser.

The Whole Truth

Coming out is a relational event that should help connect people by supplying more self-definition in order to clarify the self and relationships. It builds a relationship the same way a friend may say, "I would like to go to Spain for vacation someday." That provides new details about the self and provokes the listener to ask clarifying questions and wonder if s/he wants to rethink his/her own ideas of the ideal vacation. This adds to the relationship and provokes growth, change, and additional understanding in both participants even if they never go to Spain. Questions should be encouraged but are not easy to ask before, during, or after a drive-by coming out event.

CHAPTER 4

Into the Woods

My initial coming out experiences illustrate many of these points, including the joy and awkwardness achieved by complete lack of advance planning. For purposes of this discussion, I am thinking of coming out as simply one form of sharing one's own truth and thereby increasing self-disclosure. I came out while I was living in Stuttgart, Germany, for work. My wife and youngest daughter had recently relocated there with me from the US, and my wife volunteered to install German wireless plans on our cell phones, so I unlocked my phone and gave it to her. There she found a series of text messages I had exchanged with a man I had been flirting with when I was in the US. She confronted me, and the texts were detailed enough that there was no denying my intent. Fortunately, two colleagues from the home office had come into town that day, and leaving to take them out for the evening provided a welcomed break from the conversation at home. I knew one of the men is gay and quickly learned that the other is as well—architects!

That evening, as they talked about trips and life with their boyfriends, I recognized what my heart had longed for, and I got another whiff of what came to be my truth. It was like smelling the fragrance of a garden, and I knew what I wanted to plant in mine. My past experiences, feelings, and interests just clicked and seemed to fit well in the pattern my colleagues described for me. In the subway car on the way back to their hotel, I needed to tell someone what was on my mind. I told them, stalling for a couple subway stops, that I was going to go home and tell my wife that I'm homosexual. The colleagues took it well enough, especially considering most of our previous conversations had been about construction projects, and I had just met one of them. They gave me some encouragement that I had hoped for. I still think of that awkward, unplanned subway conversation as my coming-out moment and celebrate it every year. Please note that this is not a suggested method. I basically milked encouragement out of them by defining myself inside their group. I've spoken with both of them about that unexpected end to the evening. Despite my guerilla tactics, there seems to be no hard feelings, and I believe they both know how important they were to me on a very hard day and a turning point in my life.

As the colleagues talked about their lives, it gave me clarity about my own. They weren't intending to convert me, but in the conversation, I recognized that I enjoy being with men and would probably enjoy having one as a partner. Not only did I have an opportunity to claim it for myself, but the shared information brought us closer together. Coming out is not a missionary project. The person coming out does not need to persuade or convince the listeners of anything. He or she is simply telling what is important to him or her for information, clarity and better relationship. This is very similar to how evangelical Christians are taught to relate to their religion. They are taught to listen to truth and to apply it to their own lives and to tell others what they have discovered, responding to areas of personal need. They talk of a personal relationship with Jesus, which means that they interpret truth as it applies to themselves. So some of the most conservative accept this sense of personal truth, although they use different terms. It's very similar to what my colleagues did without any missionary intent. They told me of their same-sex relationships, and I realized I needed to try that as well because I believed it would meet my needs.

Revealing this difference to one or more people is an important act of self-definition, especially if it is a large change or definitive moment, which can have many different purposes depending on the social context. The gay community celebrates this act because it takes a lot of courage to do it the first time in the face of possible rejection, and it often starts a completely different chapter in life. I did not anticipate or expect my coming out the day it happened, and on several fronts, I regret that lack of planning. As I went home, I still had no plan of what I was going to say to my wife. In general, I imagine advance planning helps in order to clarify for the self and others the thoughts that may accompany the announcement. Specific personal applications should also be clarified in the event. For example, in other instances, it may be attached to "So I'm not interested in going out with you" or the opposite, "Would you be interested in coffee sometime?" Or maybe "So Mom, I'm never going to bring home the kind of person you'd like me to settle down with" or simply "I trust you with this." I wouldn't know really because I had no plan for that second very important conversation even though it would be more complex than talking to near strangers.

I don't celebrate outing myself to my wife because it was very painful and awkward for both of us. I had no idea where the conversations would go or even what I wanted out of the conversations. I felt I owed her honesty, and I followed through on that part of our relationship. Honesty was my main purpose, not justifying the messages she had found, but clearing the air and fully revealing myself. She asked questions about relationships I had had with men in the past, not to gather information against me, but to feel she fully understood me and my new reality, as truth was revealed. I enjoyed freely explaining and confessing my feelings for these men in my past as I revealed myself to my wife. In many ways, it was tough for both of us but valuable because we both learned about each other and showed compassion and respect for each other in the process. It was a truth-sharing moment rather than a one-time, one-sided conversation as the act is sometimes portrayed.

The conversation with my wife was good from the standpoint of building truth and relationship. I started the conversation with a summary of the men I had just met for dinner and my realization that I needed a very close relationship with one or more men in my life. My truth had already expanded, and by sharing it, I brought it to her to share who I am and to inform our relationship. At this point, I wasn't even thinking about sex, but if she had been OK with me experimenting with men on the side in a full range of relationship, I probably would have been happy to stay married. I feel slightly ashamed that I never asked for consideration of that option, but it seemed such a nonstarter; there seemed little point, and that's not the direction we went as we both talked about our needs. Since I didn't have a plan, she asked, "So what does that mean for us?' She had previously told me that if I ever cheated on her, she would want a divorce. That wasn't a threat, but a matter of her own self-respect, her truth. She told me several times during our marriage that she did not feel deeply loved by me. I now understood why and knew that it could never give her the love she deserved and felt hungry to find this love which I now felt convinced was out there for me. To remain in the marriage and continue a life without deep love for both of us. seemed sad to me. We briefly discussed other options, but in the end, divorce seemed best with all cards on the table. The honesty and sharing of truth on both sides created a basis for a clear understanding and, therefore, a relatively amicable divorce and the beginning of a new type of mutually beneficial relationship as we continue to parent our two daughters and have become professional colleagues.

Handle the Truth

Just because I had a revelation of who I am does not make me the only one with a personal truth, and I soon found out that others around me also have personal truths, which needed to be considered. But as I allude to the above, coming out is more than a one- or two-time event, and in fact, it's an ongoing process. Shortly after this, I had a series of friends to tell either because I wanted to reconnect during a particularly lonely time in my life or because they had heard rumors and asked questions. Being clear to avoid misunderstandings, telling my truth continued to be important, and I was especially careful in telling any friends to whom I was in fact attracted to, as well as being their friends. If my past attraction were somehow known, coming out might seem like a come on. I was overwhelmed with the positive responses I received from most of my friends and wept deeply several times. These positive interactions brought me closer to my friends and gave me a broad perspective of the human condition.

Our first contact was usually by e-mail, and I would ask a time to talk on the phone. Phone conversations moved quickly to the point but hid the crying pretty well. I tended to be straightforward (so to speak) in these conversations, telling about my desires, my past experimentation, as well as giving some details of my current dating situation. I learned that scoring always matters for men no matter the players. Then I asked for questions. My college roommate, who is very much a family kind of guy, asked about my daughters primarily. The best man at my wedding and I got into a deep theological discussion since that was our primary connection in our friendship. I had thought through my response to religion, so I fortunately had answers to his questions, and the discussion helped confirm many of the things I had been thinking. His acceptance and care for me confirmed that spirituality really can be about love. This built my truth in new directions. Each friend asked about my truth in ways they needed to relate to it. That's how important truth is communicated and how relationship is built.

Really?

Let me pause for a minute to describe my past relationship with my college roommate as an example of being completely ignorant of my truth. We met the first year in college as transfer students to a four-year school. At first, we each had separate roommates. He had a nice car, and our first adventure was to go grocery shopping together. It was a wild ride in a town new to both of us, as we felt the freedom of being away from home and the exhilaration of new adventures and a new friend. He was the one I referred to above as feeling like a couple in the larger group. I'd become used to the feeling of falling deeply for a male friend. Now I know it feels a lot like falling in love. As our completely platonic friendship progressed, I found myself jealous of his time away from me. I must have been needy enough about it that one day he brought me a hand-copied poem in Spanish about the importance of friendship and a promise of loyalty for an honest and sincere friend since he was a Spanish major, and I'd taken up Spanish in part because of him. I'm pretty sure my roommate was and still is very straight, as advertised by the Kelly McGillis poster he put up in our dorm room the next year. I put a temporary mustache on Kelly, I suppose, somewhat out of jealousy. He is a very sincere and empathetic man, and I think he was just responding to me as a human being. I was completely in love with him in all but name. How could I not tell from all this that I was and am totally and completely gay? But I didn't have a way of looking at my own truth to realize what it was because I was too focused on fitting my thoughts and feelings into categories acceptable in my society. Definitions have never held much appeal for me, but I think I lacked event the words to describe my feelings.

Coming out to my daughters was a long process in itself. We still have not finished and continue to check in with one another and to clarify our needs, feelings, and relationship. I prepared ahead for those conversations, thinking through things I could clarify up front to avoid anxiety. We told them about the divorce at the same time, and their bigger concerns were how to continue relationships with both parents and how to deal with the loss of a sense of family. We let the youngest daughter choose where to live, and she decided to live with me in Germany. The oldest was already in university, and my pre-prepared answers to her concerns about family unfortunately deflated into so many ineffective fatherly bromides. We've rebuilt those answers since then, and we have a growing relationship. I later asked if she wanted to hear anything about my dating life, and she politely declined, commenting that she already heard too much about her mother's dating life. I told my daughters more about myself than they probably wanted to know, but I fully became a person to them rather than only filling a role as their father.

These conversations do not have a set goal or predetermined end point. Occasionally, I think we are arriving at an important point in our relationship as our interaction takes on a form I have seen or think I understand from somewhere else, but again an external definition is not helpful as we find our way forward in relationship. Christmas seems to be the impossibly high hurdle with my daughters that I want to overcome in my new gay life. My former wife and I agreed to alternate years with the girls for Christmas. Two years ago, we were going to celebrate at my oldest daughter's house, but when I suggested bringing my boyfriend, they emphatically told me no. I felt sad as part of me felt unwelcomed. This year, the celebration was at my place, and I started socializing the idea with them early to have a friend over to share the day after Christmas with us to participate in our rather unique ritual of throwing porcelain cups into the river. They accepted this idea, and it seemed a good one since I was more of a gay mentor to this younger guy than a boyfriend. Now my sights are on two Christmases from now when I expect I will likely be married and will not give up either the daughters or my man for Christmas day. So the best option seems to let them develop a sense of family with him long before Christmas day, respecting all truths well in advance as a way of getting what I eventually want: a happy, inclusive Christmas.

In several parts of my process, I offered the truth I had, and it helped me find more. I think that is the real lesson of my coming out. Offered truth and respect leads to more truth and respect. Growing and fertilizing truth is the process of taking out our truth and looking it over with the help of someone else. Together you can pick the best spots to prune to allow new growth, and the interaction allows both to get new ideas of things they want to grow and do in their garden and new ways of working together.

Dishonesty Is Such a Lonely Word

I need go on to say a few words about the importance of honesty to the truth you know. Aside from examples like that of my roommate, when I didn't know myself well, we need to be completely honest with those with whom we share truth to the extent we know it. Before I came out to my wife, she knew I was attracted to men and knew that I sometimes visited a gay dating website. Heck, it was quite the family scandal when my daughter found the website in the computer browsing history. But I hid and lied what I had been doing there. My wife had deep suspicions about my relationship with a man whom I claimed to be just a friend, whom I had actually met on the site. She asked me many questions about that relationship. I had never had sex with him, although I wanted to badly, and at one point even planned a week away together; but since I had been unsuccessful, I could "honestly" deny "any sex with that man." But that didn't speak to my desire to have sex with him or several others I had met online.

Truth in the sense I mean it here is not in the words but in the intentions and desires of our hearts. That is the thing that must be shared. Sure, as Bill Clinton learned, the definition of *is* doesn't count as truth. Truth can, of course, be dressed up for the right audience. I don't talk about my sex life with my daughters, but purposely hiding the big picture of who we are does no one any good. For my daughters, I even go as far as to annotate my personal journals, knowing that someday after I'm gone, they may read my diaries. I write things like "Gentle reader, please skip to the next page. There's only an orgy on this page." First, dishonesty disconnects us from others and erodes trust when discovered. While I was fooling around with men while still living with my wife, I lived two lives, effectively splitting myself in half. Talking about our life experiences makes them richer for the teller and connects to the listener through the act of honesty, if not identification.

I had two lives that could not communicate with each other, leaving me much less opportunity for connection with others. I didn't tell the person closest to me about the deepest passion in my life, and

I certainly didn't tell the men stories about my wife and kids. I got into the habit of taking off my wedding ring when I saw the friend I was lusting over. He knew I was married and could see the ring mark on my finger. He asked me to be honest with him at one point and not worry about the ring. I suppose I wanted to keep an illusion of control. That's why I didn't tell my wife. I feared that we would lurch toward some conclusion that I couldn't control and wouldn't like. My family was important to me, and I didn't want to lose it. That was my fear. And I told myself that I would never tell her because it would hurt her. That was a nice, convenient lie for myself, and my truth stayed stunted. The result of this deception was years of living a split and disconnected life away from my truth or me. My lies did not change the end result, and the end state was basically the same as if I had told my wife earlier. For her, it resulted in the worst possible situation to break up in: having just left everything and everyone in the US, I outed myself, precipitating a change in the relationship in a place where she knew no one and had no means of self-support. It was a disaster and hurt our relationship as people.

Deceit creates distance. And I lost years of living my true self. Honest and open sharing of truth promotes growth like cross-pollination. By contrast, I had a great relationship in Stuttgart with a hetero friend who wanted to hear all the details of my sexual adventures. I think, for him, it was a way to live vicariously and remember his past when he had more freedom to play the field. For me, sharing the experiences made them more enjoyable and gave a great excuse to spend time with a new friend. Men really are dogs.

Sometimes growth becomes more intense as the foliage responds to the environment. Sun, rain, and wind can all move growth forward. The relationship with Kae, my youngest who lived with me, and the arrangement gave more opportunity to wait for and adapt to her reactions and questions; and for that reason, I've probably built a better post-coming-out relationship with her than anyone else. For me, it was liberating to express and to show my true self and to receive positive reactions. As I started to date men, Kae set rules for me and did things like dictate a curfew for my return home each night after a date and required me to call when I would be late as a mirror of the boundaries I set for her. However, she sometimes felt uncomfortable with a stranger in the house. More on that story in a moment.

Truth Trouble

I would be remiss if I left the impression that coming out and telling one's truth is only easy. Every truth seems to have a certain need to be absolute and unquestioned, and that is true of personal truth as well. One friend and his wife sent me multiple messages highlighting their beliefs that being gay and getting divorced were breaking the more generally perceived sense of truth and morality. Our families had become close friends, where everyone had a good friend in the other family. I think my friend's reaction was so strong largely because he felt he had lost our relationship. Our families had integrated closely, and the divorce completely messed that up. The messages over several months implied or stated that I must be the one out of step and that my truth was no truth at all. The messages hurt quite a bit, but over time, I was also able to understand that he still wanted to be my friend.

Our friendship has become more individually focused, and despite the kind invitation to host me whenever in town, I know that I will feel uncomfortable spending time with his family alone. I offered to host their son and friends as they came through Europe, and it was nice to continue the former kindnesses between the families as I could, and I know they continue trying to do so for me. I also believe that friendships of every kind are worth preserving, and kindness is always welcome. Every private truth will face criticism from other truths. That's just the nature of truths and the people who hold them. It's important to stay calm and remind one's self of what is true for you, to explain that truth, and to make modifications if needed, but respect yourself and your truth and that of others. Beware: absolute truth also corrupts absolutely and leads to conflict.

Ongoing discussions with friends who believe exclusively in eternal, didactic truth led me to write the apologia in the appendix as a formal theological response.

I have to often remind myself to be tolerant of other truths as well. For example, I have to confess that I don't understand drag performers. I dated and lived with pretty, feminine partners most of my life, so I'm quite sure that I don't need more of the same. I'm attracted to other men because they are masculine, so dressing up as a woman holds little attraction for me. I have come to understand the showmanship from my experience with theater, and by listening, I also understand that some queens desire to publicly reject convention. I get that too, but I need to be conscious of these different perspectives to help me accept these other truths.

My most difficult relationship where I have to keep explaining myself and revealing my truth to a sometimes unreceptive audience is with my father. I think this relationship best illustrates the importance of growing one's own truth and how to deal with others who believe they have the Truth of one kind or another. My father is not a particularly macho man, nor is he ashamed of me or my gayness. Quite to the contrary, my most embarrassing moments of growing up came because of how proud my dad was of me. He would tell people about some little thing I did or said as if I was amazing. He continues this practice into my adulthood, but he just never includes my gayness as one of the things he is proud of. His truth comes straight (double meaning OK) out of the Bible as he understands it and believes that homosexuality is wrong. He never questions that the Bible is the absolute Word of God. His truth is a transplant. When I first came out as gay, I mostly got silence. Then came the period where I kind of provoked him to talk. I was still in Germany at the time, so I would lob a bombshell such as e-mailing him about my dating life or dropping hints about my boyfriend, and then I'd wait for the next e-mail or phone call to get his response after he had time to think. I understand his dilemma. The son he loves had a different truth than he did. It's hard to enjoy either or both together in the cognitive dissonance.

I certainly felt that when my daughter didn't like my boyfriend hanging around. So to get through the silence, I provoked him into some conversation, and it would pull open the door a bit for us to exchange some of ourselves and share some of our truth with each other on a haphazard, somewhat aggressive basis. I don't know if he thought of himself as lobbing bombs back, but sometimes the impact felt like it. He would tell me the Bible lesson he was thinking of for the day and relate it to me. Usually in the story, I was the evildoer who had gone astray. I found an e-mail the other day where he called me to the Prodigal Son who had rejected everything his Father had given. I had left the correct path to live a selfish lifestyle. I called my dad on it and asked if that means he can never accept me as a homosexual and that he'll always treat my boyfriend like a passing phase that will hopefully go away. Throwing hand grenades is not a fun game when someone throws them back, but it can get the juices flowing when a relationship seems stuck.

Some exchange is better than none, I suppose. By mutual agreement, we settled down to a more productive way to exchange ideas. In one of our messages, I referred to the play *Death of a Salesman* by Arthur Miller, which I knew he had read in college and explained one of my takeaways from the play. He said that my interpretation explained more than he had ever gotten in college. He previously alluded to wanting to do something together, so I suggested that we read *Death of a Salesman* together, and I would prepare some discussion notes to help him prepare each week. He liked the idea very much and we did it, with weekly play discussions by phone. I used to teach theater and English, so making a study guide was easy, and I found I was pretty good at guessing how much reading and ambiguity my dad could handle each week. I learned some wonderful things about my dad, like how he had always wanted to be an airline pilot, but didn't quite make it. We talked about big dreams and his philosophies about sales. I didn't think ahead, however, to the heavy family conflict content near the end of the play when one of the children, Biff, exclaimed, "We never told the truth in this house for one minute!" That started some provocative discussion. *Death of a Salesman* is not the answer to all gay-straight relationships, but it's an example of finding something to do together that allowed two different people to come together to casually and easily share big truth with each other.

There is far too much bomb throwing in the world already, much of it with the intent to do great harm. Unfortunately, this is often the response to someone having a different Truth, which is perceived as a threat and "The other Truth and the infidel who cultivates it must be destroyed." How much better to find a forum to gently, humanely, and respectfully share thoughts and truth together. If we lived in the same town and actually liked sports, maybe Dad and I would have gone bowling instead. The activity doesn't matter, but the opportunity does. For us, the play was the thing to pull us deeper into discussion. The individual who holds a different truth needs to guard his or her garden from attackers, cultivate it with reverence, and share the produce with all who are willing and accepting. I think that all believers in truth can do the same. It doesn't hurt me that my father shares Sunday school lessons with me. He's done it my whole life anyway. I welcome his sharing of what he thinks and believes. That's relationship. It's interesting to see where his mind goes for application sometimes, and in that way, I learn more about him. I question and challenge his conclusions as needed and sometimes have to set boundaries. We accept each other that way and strengthen our respect, our truths, and our relationship in the process. That is the ultimate good in having different truths.

The same sort of steps and obstacles apply in other sorts of coming out moments that are not necessarily about sexuality. While I have been treading water at work in my new job, I recently told my boss about my extreme frustration with my position. In this case, I was better prepared and sent him an e-mail that previewed some issues and ideas of the types of things I would prefer and have more talent for. That gave him time to assess and sort options, and I was correct in believing that, between us, we could find a way for me to stay in the same office with some change in expectations and goals. The most difficult part is that he continually wanted to define my perspective in narrow terms he understood, and I had to regularly redirect us to a descriptive view of the solution I envisioned. We still have more work to do to match me with work that needs to be done, but we are both on the lookout for options with a similar understanding of the parameters.

CHAPTER 5

Identifying Personal Truth

After coming out of the closet or stepping out from the crowd in any sort of self-definition, the next step is to learn how and what you want more of now that you step away from that which you want less. What will your truth garden look like? There's two ways to learn what you want to grow: to look around and to meet people. You'll know your truth when you see it and as pieces start fitting together.

The first step in finding your truth is to know what it looks like. Your truth is made up of parts of you, specifically your needs, your abilities, and your perceptions. I found a lot of truth for me in the Christopher Street Day (gay pride) celebrations in Germany and attended as many as I could in various cities. The German celebrations take their name from Christopher Street, the site of the Stonewall riots in the US. I don't doubt that Germans were influenced to decriminalize homosexuality that same year because of the riots in the US, but I find it curious that these American events so strongly impacted the naming of the event. Christopher Street events generally attract several thousand participants to a weekend of street food and drinks, music on several stages, and a parade. In Germany, the event brings in the entire gay community to central attractions and events, which take over the center of town, like so many other German street festivals. I attended my first Christopher Street Day (CSD) in Köln (Cologne), second only to Berlin for the size of its gay community and not far from Stuttgart. Unlike pride events in other parts of the world, Germans do not hold all the festivals on the same day but have a season of Christopher Street Day events up and down the country. This allows the best performers to make it to many events and the crowds from out of town follow. In Cologne and elsewhere, I became immediately attracted by and a bit jealous of the openness with which men were able to publicly show affection for one another. Over time, CSD festivals became my cathedrals of acceptance and self-acceptance. That is personal truth, not that I'm the only one with said truth, but it's personal to me.

In large part because of these experiences, showing affection and consideration for a partner have always been very important to me, as well as openness and freedom from shame to show one's own truth As a result, holding hands in public became an important part of all my relationships with men. A sense of community and inclusion permeated the CSD crowds, which my values found very attractive. So the differences in local culture along with acceptance were especially intoxicating for me. The first evening, I found a picnic bench where I could watch the crowd, and there I sat to eat my dinner. A lesbian couple came through the crowd, and one of the pair pulled her partner toward me. They sat across from me, and the puller began an animated conversation, "Are you here by yourself?" "Don't you want a partner?" (Ouch, that hurt!) "What's your name?" I told her, and she continued, "You seem like a pretty great guy, Andrew. So what you need to do is go into that crowd and announce eloquently, 'I am Andrew!' (as she demonstrated some highbrow elocution) and you'll find someone wonderful who thinks you're wonderful too. I am sure." I didn't take her dating advice literally, but I did appreciate the vote of confidence, and in time, I saw the merit in her suggested approach.

Later that evening, I attended a candlelight memorial for AIDS victims, and a group of young guys stood in front of me, playing with their candles, occasionally smashing their drinking glasses on purpose or by accident as they engaged in horseplay with one another. I watched their antics with growing amusement until several of the guys saw me watching and laughing up my sleeve. I got a friendly nod from several, and they went back to their fun. Toward the end of the ceremony, everyone was supposed to link arms and sing together. One of the group leaders turned around and pulled me into the group to link arms with them. He introduced himself as Adrian and introduced his boyfriend, also Adrian. I linked arms between the two Adrians and sang song after song, including "Major Tom," the unofficial anthem of German nonconformity. The guys were impressed I knew the words, and I was impressed that anyone under thirty years old had even heard of the song. It was wonderful to be included and considered. These two encounters at the CSD crystalized parts my truth and helped define my values; inclusion is important, consideration of others—especially strangers—is important, and I learned that I'm an acceptable human being as a gay man. I'm very sure Adrian and Adrian as well as the lesbian couple and many others at the event share these values, but they became my truth because I witnessed, selected, and digested the truth myself. The realization came as part of processes already going on inside me rather than having it preached at me or imposed by a group.

By contrast, there are a few things that personal truth is not, and these are also worth noting. Someone else does not explain it to us. I explain my truth here as an example of how an individual finds personal truth. It is not intended that it should be your truth as well. You may find a truth similar to my truth, but mine is not required in order to be a happy homosexual. Some kind of personal truth is required, but not necessarily mine. Sort of by definition, someone else's truth is not your personal truth. It is not a set of rules or norms required to fit into a particular group. There are many groups like this in the world, including gay groups. A motorcycle group such as Dykes on Bikes, for example, likely has certain expectations of how its members respond to the outside world, especially activities that are traditionally masculine or feminine, and likely has some expectations of about members' ability to ride and interest in motorcycles. I've been in social groups of gay men where everyone speaks, looks, and reacts the same. That is a group norm, not a personal truth, and in those cases, I use my intercultural communication skills to understand the meaning behind what to me seems like show, and I continue to be myself. As Rick Clemons stresses in the book *Frankly My Dear, I'm Gay*, "If you're not careful, you'll end up stepping out of one closet and right into another." Personal truth needs to guide you rather than group norms or dogma.

Space to Grow

A person newly out or with any new truth must also allow him- or herself time and mental space to experiment and try new things within the limit of good sense, advice, and support. A person seeking to grow their truth needs to find experiences and people from whom they could get some idea of what is and is not important to that truth. Especially as a single dad, I needed a huge amount of freedom to step away from that role and better learn who I am and space to grow to find where and what to include into my truth. Stuttgart is a big, exciting palace with many opportunities for adventure. A person in transition should try new things with as little self-criticism as possible. Any place with a large number of people among whom to find friends and organizations to try out will do. Two saunas in Stuttgart are a major part of the gay scene there and great places to meet men. However, growing up near San Francisco during the initial outbreak of AIDS, I had picked up a prejudice against such places as seedy hotbeds of disease. I gave myself permission and a regular regime of testing and began to experiment. My big motivator was to find a man with whom I could build a happy partnership, and I met many potential candidates in the saunas relatively quickly. With time, I learned that saunas per se are not nearly as dangerous as my lack of caution in exciting situations.

I have since begun to somewhat question the value of sex as a means to start a relationship. While it is extremely enjoyable, that level of enjoyment makes it difficult to expand the relationship because it feels risky to move into a different aspect of the coupling. Taking off on the infamous friend zone, I've found myself stuck several times in the fuck-buddy zone, where one or both of us enjoys the sex so much that he doesn't want to put it at risk by suggesting something more. For me, the sex was enjoyable, but almost immediately, I started thinking about longer-term relationship. Internally at cross-purposes, I found myself often feeling disappointed and stuck. So a strong dose of sex may not be the ideal start to a relationship for me.

There's two ways to go about gay dating. The first is to look in places where you know you'll find other gays, such as gay bars, resorts, and online. The other option is to pursue groups with similar interests to your own and to discover other gays there. I tried both methods. I joined a local theater group, thinking I might find a gay man with whom I shared a hobby. I met two very nice gay men, but both already had partners. They proved to be quite supportive and encouraging in my quest, so I had a very positive outcome, but no partner. Until you know a person of interest is gay, however, the first step in securing a date or more intimate conversation in a mixed group is nerve-wracking and rather awkward. One cute man in the theater group caught my attention, but after a few weeks of loosely hanging out at rehearsals, I realized he had mentioned a girlfriend several times. I asked a few more questions before I became more direct and potentially made a fool of myself.

Gay hangouts have the opposite problems. It's easy to become attached quickly and then realize that you and the person of interest have little in common They are also too predictable, so predators lurk there waiting to exploit the unsuspecting. I've especially found this dangerous online. I fit a demographic, and several younger men assume I am a lonely older man who will gladly part with money for a little attention. I can't believe the number of declarations of undying love I received from young guys I'd never met who desperately wanted to live with me, especially from Eastern Europe or Africa. Their plan usually involved me paying all expenses for them to come to the West. Sometimes I blew off the advance right away and even mocked a few of the most obvious appeals for money. I let others stroke my ego for a while, but I wasn't above totally falling for a few of them. Maybe they were genuine, or maybe they just knew the right buttons to push. For one man, I bought presents and had already planned a trip for him to see me before I noticed he wasn't interested in me, my Truth, or who I am. One night, I told him about a great milestone I had achieved at work, but he downplayed the whole thing because he didn't see any monetary reward for me. That was too materialistic for my taste.

My advice is to fully expose your truth to any potential partner, and the response will be very telling. That truth needs to be more than simply what you like. That only gives a con artist more clues of what to use as bait, but instead, use lots of talk about the things that interest you and represent your values with a space for response. I often talked about interesting interactions with people during the day, art, and big ideas. I once invited a guy who seemed interested in art and architecture to a museum for a date, He declined and said he'd prefer to just have sex. The response surprised and intrigued me, but I knew with whom I was dealing. One of the great things about Truth is that it often brings out the truth in others. Consider the options of where to meet friends and lovers, then freely share your truth, and the people you meet seem to sort themselves. I suppose this is my more modest version of going forth and declaring "I am Andrew" in anticipation that someone will be attracted.

A Little Help from My Friends

Growing one's own truth is not a loner sport. And fellow travelers should be welcomed on the journey, especially if they have a unique perspective. One group that I found extremely helpful to my journey was in Stuttgart's Sport Verein, a gay men's sports organization. I didn't play many traditional sports, but I did a semester of ballroom dancing with them. It was so wonderful to see gay couples interact with one another and to talk to some of them about their experiences. Several, like me, had no partner or a partner uninterested in dancing, so it gave opportunity to talk about problem-solving and gave me the chance to meet a great dance partner. The group shared many good times. Since ballroom dance is mostly designed around gender roles, it was fun to see the group, and each couple divide themselves into those who would lead and who would follow. Then on a cultural note, as a remnant of World War II, the word *der Fuehrer* (the leader) is still a dirty word, and one night, a substitute instructor almost had an entire gym full of adult men reduced to helpless giggles as he kept accidently using the German F-word.

So far, I've discussed methods through which I found and confirmed my truth in reaction to circumstances. These are important steps, but proactively growing one's truth is the theme of this book. Choosing to have friends with similar truth is an essential, active element to growing one's truth, and the similarity increases comfort and applicability of the truth learned. Being exposed to their truth raises new issues that confirm what one is already doing or suggests additional issues for consideration and possible addition to one's own truth. I discovered a wonderful set of gay friends at work whom I collectively and affectionately refer to as the pink posse. The way they interacted with one another and the world around them gave me encouragement and ideas of things that were important or unimportant to me, helping me to grow and expand. I rarely set out to imitate any of them, but reacting to their truth helped me identify my own.

My first experience came as I got to know one of the guards at work. It turned out that he had also attended the CSD festival in Cologne alone, just like I did, and I could see that I wasn't as insane as I occasionally felt that weekend or in the months afterward. He is about twenty-five years younger than me, but we were both very new to coming out and looking for our place in the gay world. It was a very comforting relationship, as we shared notes about finding our first boyfriends and what we expect or hope for in a relationship. We double-dated a few times. My favorite interactions happened when he started complaining about all the time he had wasted pretending to be heterosexual, and I would remind him that he'd have at least twenty-five years more than I would to be gay, so I didn't want to hear any complaints. Such interactions reminded me of the value of each day, the importance in each relationship, and the shortness of time. I came out at age fifty, so compared to him, I really had no time to waste. It was also interesting to watch him fit a fairly macho persona and a macho work environment into being gay, and the way his boyfriend played off this persona gave me lots of thought about gender expectations and roles.

Two other friends, Matt and Stergis, were complete opposites in style, but both were part of this friend group. Listening to their ceaseless banter over lunch helped me find a style of interaction that works best for me. Matt was more analytical and down-to-earth and sometimes played the role of my protector, while Stergis was more emotive, trying to always get me excited about something new. By nature, I was somewhat more like Matt, but occasionally at lunch, I would try on Stergis's energetic, breezy speech patterns. It wasn't a good fit for me, and while I would often see Matt go toe-to-toe with him in the same style, I just didn't have the energy or passion to keep up.

Matt's steadiness and similarity to my core nature gave me a great idea. One day, I had him alone for lunch, and I asked Matt if he would be my gay big brother. Even though he was more than ten years younger than me, the deal would be this: I could ask him any stupid question I had about being gay, sort of like stereotypical little brothers ask questions about sex. He had the right at any time to slap me upside the head, like a typical big brother, and tell me to mind my own business, but there were no penalties on either side, so I came to depend on him to tell me his whole truth and we would still be brothers.

The designation as brothers also made it intentionally clear that we would never ever be romantic with each other, although we were very close. He has a good partner. Our relationship cleared up many pressing issues for me. I mostly had questions about how he met his partner and how he knew he was the one and his thoughts about an open versus a monogamous relationship. Matt kindly opened his truth for me to question and understand, and while I did not always come to the same conclusions, Matt's truth and his reasoning helped me choose seeds with which to grow my own truth. This relationship kept me sane through several tough times. When I was in the hospital, he volunteered to be gay uncle Matt and look in on my daughter. He also was a great sounding board through several relationships. His most memorable advice was "No time for stupid boys." I could tell Matt freely about my truth, whatever that might be, and his reaction sometimes helped me through important course corrections. We both have fathers with difficulty adjusting to our truths, and we shared encouragement and invaluable suggestions. Every gay man needs to find a gay big brother like Matt. Every gay man needs to look for opportunities to be a big brother like Matt. Those going through a life transition must find friends to talk, get ideas from, and bounce off ideas with.

About Town

A good example of the confirmation function of friends happened when I would bring a date to the group or tell them about my latest. It was not that I cared whether they approved or disapproved. That wasn't the point, but telling others what I like about a man was another way to share my truth and helped me understand and accept or correct my perception and it was a very personal act with which I entrusted them, and being friends, they did not disappoint. I introduced the man who later became my first important boyfriend to the group at a Christmas market. It's a rather informal event in Germany's long line of seasonal street-food festivals. It's easy to wander off and do your own thing if the group is not engaging, and group participants have to work to even be physically colocated, let alone talk. In this environment, I could see Matt working hard to get to know my man, Beni, while Beni was sticking with the group and asking me to translate key English phrases he missed. It was so affirming to see different friends in my life trying hard to understand the others, affirming different parts of my truth as a whole. I had never heard Matt use so much German, and on the way home, I was so ebullient and thankful that I kissed Matt, which is not a usual thing between us, and fortunately, his boyfriend didn't beat me up.

After returning to the US, I gained a great deal of comfort by joining an LGBT-affirming church. I was amazed to learn that it is part of a denomination of Metropolitan Community Churches, which vigorously affirm congregants with nonstandard sexualities. Having grown up in a fairly conservative environment, the return to church felt comfortable, and the acceptance that God loves me and that these people cared about me as a gay man rocked my concept of divinity, and I again found a group of like-minded individuals who did not dictate, but supported me as I filled out my truth. I gravitated to the choir because I like that sort of thing and found the antithesis of the kind of men I grew up with in church. They were more interested in designer socks than sports scores and helped me feel comfortable as the more emotional person I was becoming. The choir director was a large African American who exudes acceptance for the all individuals of the choir and encourages the group to send that acceptance out to the congregation. I felt taken care of, and my values and truth blossomed but not in the more traditional way of religious cognitive dogma, but instead in emotional honesty and acceptance. In fact, remaining dogma continued to dramatically explode in my head as religious, personal, spiritual, and sexual elements mixed in new and fascinating ways.

One Sunday, I realized the man sitting next to me in the service was holding a centerfold of a topless, very attractive man whom I enjoyed looking at too. The shoulds and should nots just no longer functioned, and so I had to throw them out. The boyfriend I met there (more about him later) and I got in the habit of kissing during part of the communion service as a symbol of our spiritual connection to each other. I continue to taunt the remaining dogma in my brain with my list of ninety-five theses such as "Did God have gay sex in mind when he created the human body? Because it is feels so amazing." For anyone looking to burn me at the stake, this paragraph should about do it. But it is not my intent to be antireligious or to denigrate a strong tradition, but to make it more inclusive of multiple perspectives. I am finding my truth that may be similar or different from that held by others, and that is the journey everyone must undertake.

A monolithic truth has little place for individual variation and so has difficulty speaking to individuals different from the core group, and so individual human dignity becomes a trade-off for group unity. It's good to worship or hang out with similar people to ourselves because we need connection to other human beings, but it is also important to develop our own understanding of truth, which makes sense to the individual and reflects his or her uniqueness. If the individual conforms to the group rather than growing personal truth, his or her uniqueness is lost. Instead of *either/or*, we need to accept the premise of *and* to see how different truths can complement, tolerate, and support one another. That is real spirituality. The first performance I did with the church choir illustrated this point. We sang at the funeral of a great gospel singer of the denomination, Dolores Berry (she has several songs on YouTube for the curious). Besides singing, the service consisted of people reflecting on their experience with this unique woman. Each speaker further blew my mind at the idea of celebrating traits so different from the WASPy morality that I was raised with, and speakers confirmed the positive impact she had on others because she did not fit the rules that I thought were so secure. Two women elaborated on Dolores's passion to share her love of soul food with inexperienced white people and would eat plate after plate to illustrate how it was done. Two of the speakers confirmed the joy she had in describing herself by singing the word *lesbian*, and person after person told of Ms. Berry's ability to look into the soul and speak to the individual's need. She could see and take care of personal need because she was free to be her own person and ignored preconceptions, which allowed her to really see.

Respect Yourself and Others Rather than the Rules

I've made some interesting observations in my journey, and while each doesn't produce a distinct value, the whole creates a worldview that colors my perceptions of that world. I don't know if this is true for other groups, but I've experienced with gay men that Truth flows more easily just before and after sex. I once invited a handsome policeman to my apartment, and as we lay spent on the bed, he started talking about his open relationship with his girlfriend, who also experimented with same-sex relationships. We talked about feelings and needs, and I shared a surprising amount of my story. The sudden intimacy was amazing and came at an unexpected time. I was taught that one should only have sex after a close connection had been established. But experimental truth seemed to confirm the opposite. In the same way, I first met a good friend (not from work) by having sex with him at a gay sauna. Afterward, he talked freely about his partner, and I talked about my search for a partner. He enjoyed sex much more than his partner and had a free pass to go experiment. I enjoyed his wisdom and insight, so our times together usually offered some combination of sex and philosophy.

CHAPTER 6

Balancing with Other Truth

Despite relational constraints, one must request of others what one needs to grow his or her truth. For my first birthday with a boyfriend, I requested that my daughter Kae put her discomfort aside for the evening to hang out with my boyfriend and I for dinner and to try to make conversation. I realized how important this was to me to be open and out and to feel normal in a family setting, and I tried to help her understand. The evening went fairly well except I found myself translating between English and German for them most of the evening. I was a bit apprehensive of how she would respond to me hosting my boyfriend overnight for the first time, but I told her in advance what I was planning, left time for questions, and got through it fairly well.

That first night, as we were in bed, she returned home after being out with her friends. One friend needed to use our restroom, so he came in the apartment in some confidence because Kae knew we would be out of sight, in the bedroom, with the door closed. Clear understanding helps a great deal to settle relationships and gives room to grow truth. As they passed in front of the bedroom, I heard my daughter tell her friend to keep quiet because I was in there with my boyfriend. The friend replied, "That's so cool that your dad's gay." For a while, I really relished being the cool gay dad, with my truth fully hanging out. Over the next month, Kae invited several friends over to the apartment who were questioning their own sexuality, and I hope our example of a family at peace with our truths comforted them in their own journeys. The highlight of this period was when I invited my daughter to a nearby CSD festival (in Germany, the festivals take place throughout the month of June). She responded with enthusiasm and asked if she could invite one of her questioning friends as well. I was glad to have them both along and to share such an important part of my well-being. They spent most of the day hunting Pokémon but also experienced the acceptance of the event, passively sharing my truth. Kae's friend did not feel like a stranger but a fellow traveler whom we could help to find his way, and I even coached him on ways to ask his parents' permission to go with us in the first place, which was very satisfying and comforting in living out my truth by accepting his.

Simply living without shame is good for the soul. Of course, being a parent never stays easy, despite the occasional illusion of coming to a safe conclusion. When I finally found a man I wanted to settle down with and asked him to move in with me, my daughter was quite upset and argued that she could not be herself at home with two men in the house, feeling like she needed to always be presentably dressed rather than casual. We talked through each of our perspectives but could not find a solution. It eventually seemed best to both of us for her to live with her mother, at least for a while. I was no longer the cool gay dad and went back to just being gay and a dad. Anyway, one should never rely on the opinion of teenagers for a sense of self-esteem. This setback saddened me, as my relationship with my daughter became a bit more distant, but my truth was intact, as was hers. The proof of truth telling is not that we always get what we want, but that integrity and beauty remain.

Flings and Flakes

A nonsynchronous response can come in many forms. I don't know if I can generalize these next comments to all gay men, but it is certainly true in Germany. During my short time back in the

US, it seemed these behaviors are common there as well. A lesbian friend also commented that some of these traits also arise in that community. Maybe it's a human trait, but it's worth a comment here.

In my brief initial emergence into gay dating, I could not believe the high percentage of dates where we felt enough connection to make future plans and even to talk like a couple, but then the other guy didn't follow up or simply ditched me. In the US, it's called ghosting and is extremely discouraging, and I caution anyone newly coming out not to take such behavior personally. It's too common and happened to me over and over again. I had met the guy who provided my first example online shortly before I left Stuttgart for medical treatment. During my time away, we communicated a bit, and at my return, he was very interested to get together again. That was a good date, and we felt a degree of connectedness, as he did some daring behavior to flirt and catch my attention, and I fawned over him in return. We agreed on a second date with a specific plan to come to my place and make dinner together on a specific night, but as the day came closer, I heard nothing from him and got no confirmation that we were still on. He never texted and never showed. He did reply several weeks later to say that he had some cellphone issues, but he never came looking for more. I've since learned a Spanish word for this kind of guy: *barajo*.

I think the most extreme example of disappearing (and this may be specifically a gay man thing) was a guy I met at a sauna. I felt like we had a real connection, and I'm pretty sure he was one of the most gorgeous humans I have ever seen naked. But as soon as we had finished with sex, he seemed to be looking for excuses to slip away. We went downstairs for a shower and eventually decided to go back upstairs for more sex. He said he'd follow me upstairs, but never did, and I never saw him again. He loved being sought after, and I was sure I met that need for him in our original encounter, but I think he got cold feet as I hinted at a more enduring relationship. He was simply distracted by the presence of other men desiring him in the sauna. I teased him about his behavior, but it was so engrained that he rolled off excuses pretty quickly.

People, their spirits, their hopes, and their desires are important to me. Our mutual lust was delicious, but being only tied to the physical seemed wrong to me. So while I understood his need and perspective, I couldn't say we shared much truth together, so for me that would be little basis for a relationship except lots of sex. So rather than simply judging him against my standard, I was aware that we could have very little together as a valuable relationship. I am not going to cut out an ethic of right and wrong, but in a practical sense, sharing truth seems important for a relationship of any significance. Let me jump ahead for a minute to Luis, the man I plan to marry.

In our first date, Luis listened attentively to me about difficulties I was having in life and showed real empathy. By the second date, he told me about helping out his sister and her family, and we got rather excited together in talking about helping others. At one point, I remember that he exclaimed, "If you can't do good, what good are you?" At that moment, I fell in love with him in identifying this common trait. Luis and I have still not had sex, but we have similar values that hold us together. As a matter of respect for the relationship I was still in when I met him and the circumstances of being separated for months after we fell in love, we have not had the opportunity to be intimate. But I contrast these two relationships to show how both men seemed attractive, but note that sex was not as strong a motivation as similar truth to make a lasting impression or relationship. I would have loved to have sex with the sauna man regularly and often, but for me, I realized that would not have given me the kind of relationship I want and need. More about Luis at the end. I don't think the happy ending was going to be a surprise, but now it definitely will not be. Sorry. There will be some heroism, drama, and saving the gay boy from his high and lonely tower at the end, if that is any future consolation.

CHAPTER 7

Toward a Happy Ending

I need to talk a bit about my first serious gay relationship with Beni because it illustrates three important approaches to an unknown future, which I think is the biggest worry of anyone who does not fit in with the crowd. It is a serious challenge to any idea of truth. These three are sort of a classic trinity: faith, hope, and love. While people sometimes use them interchangeably, the differences between these concepts are important.

Your truth is what you make it, and to me, Beni was a wonderful potential life partner whom I met almost four years ago now, shortly after coming out. However, the stars did not align around that relationship, although it had a wonderful start. We met at a gay bar called the Stall (couldn't ask for a more romantic name, right?). Beni liked to claim that he saw me first, and I'd give him that because I noticed him because he kept staring at me. That doesn't happen for me very often. So we played around in a dark corner and then hung out at the bar for several hours. He'd come to the bar with friends, one of whom was his ride, so I stayed with him even past being tired as we waited for his friend to be ready to go. I've never yawned so much on a date and still see the guy on subsequent occasions. I got his number, and we worked over the next several months to better know each other. He's originally from the former Yugoslavia and grew up in Italy, so I loved going to Italian restaurants with him in Stuttgart and watching him get his Italian macho on and order around the waitstaff. The downside was that he's friends with every Italian in town, so the waitstaff also felt free to hang out and chat. Beni once told me, "At least at this place, they don't pull up a chair to your table." So if we had something serious to talk about, we went for Thai.

In six months, we grew important truths together, and truth telling and growing were always important. It seemed like the sun shone down and revealed this wonderful man to me in radiant glory. He seemed exactly who I needed at exactly the right time. I think some of the strong infatuation came because I liked him, and he liked me, which is strong reassurance after recently coming out of the closet. I think many homosexuals feel as I did, that I was unsure if I would ever, ever find someone in this new world whom I would find so alluring and who would actually like me in return. In short, Beni shone out amazingly brightly and gave me great hope that I could in fact find a long-term relationship with him or that the possibility in fact was real with someone. I had fallen in love several times after I came out, but rarely did the other man feel something so close in return with such intensity. We spoke German together, a non-native language for both of us. Beni agreed to read this book as one of his early English lessons. So I dreaded the need to explain epistemology in German, but I have since learned that it's basically the same word.

The relationship, however, was hard to define, and Beni frequently corrected me as I tried to give it a name. I'm not sure if it was because I didn't understand the nuance in German or if my ideas were just different than his. The point of having a relationship is not having it or defining it, but the opportunities it gives to live one's truth in a safe environment and to watch it grow under the care of another person's acceptance. I learned so much with were both rather shocked, but I couldn't let go. He asked me why, and I told him all I had imagined that we could be together and asked if we could discuss alternatives to the end that the company's action had forced upon us. Finally, we hit upon on a plan that he would seek a company transfer to the US, near where I would live, or take a Christmas vacation and come to visit me. We ended my return visit to Stuttgart in unknown territory, and had little clue how or if we would be together again. We then said that we will always love the other, and, at the same time, released each other from any promise of a future relationship. Our relationship moved online. We stayed close through the process of sharing our Truths. Sharing has that effect even though what we had to share were frequently negative feelings. I had an ongoing need to understand that he really loved me after the neglect of the visit. Beni still seemed excited about the prospect to come to the US. I also continued to meet men in the US and kept in contact with several others I had met in Stuttgart. I hoped someday I would get a chance to get to know Beni on a consistent, daily basis and decide if I wanted to be with him the rest of my life. That was a wonderful vision, but I couldn't let it be the only possible scenario under which I feel like I got what I needed.

CHAPTER 8

Faith and Hope

Hope and faith are essential elements in a relationship, but these are not rigid constructs, and we must leave ourselves flexibility for changing circumstances. There's a world of men who can be excellent partners and give me the connection that I crave. I wanted more than anything to find one who is in love with me too. I knew Beni, and we had a good start, and I also had strong possibilities with several others. In those final weeks together, I learned to accept my partner's need to do well at work, and I still felt hurt by his distance and seeming lack of need for time with me and long wondered if he was more interested in coming to the US to look for a job rather than in a relationship with me. That was my truth and my deep questioning of it. Beni being the one was not truth but one possibility. With this perspective on how to handle an unknown future, I will wrap up the end of this story for readers.

In my loneliness in the new city and wonderful memories of Beni, I invited him to come live with me in the US. However, his company was facing tough economic realities and had curtailed the international transfer of employees. Beni contacted me with his suggestion that he come privately to the US and we marry right away so that he could have status to work. To me, that sounded like a huge commitment, given my uncertainty about how he felt about me. Any time to evaluate the relationship had evaporated. When Beni heard my objections, he wrapped himself in feeling offended and withdrew, saying there's no need to contact him in the future. I was devastated because he made no attempt to work through our problems.

This story illustrates three important elements in an approach to an unknown future. Faith is traditionally evidence of things not seen. Beni and I were overjoyed with each other right away and started talking lightly and indirectly about marriage early in our relationship. The question came to me that probably comes to all couples considering marriage: "How do I know if this will be a good partner for me in the long term?" I took up the traditional concept of faith to answer that question. When one can't see the future, one has to piece together what it might become based on evidence from the present as the only guide available. Faith is not blind, and I continued to question what I thought I knew. When Beni continued to defer and deflect requests to talk about how he really felt about me, my need for caution increased. I could see that Beni had many qualities that I could never get tired of, including intelligence, playfulness, and hard work. We had similar needs and talents in socializing with others. He also had a dream for his future that seemed very compatible with mine. I had lots of evidence that we could resolve problems together, which was an important skill for a long-term relationship, and we really liked each other. But I also had to be honest with myself that I had some concerns like his inability to talk about emotions or connect with me to deal with mine. This area became a redline for me when he wouldn't talk, and when he couldn't satisfactorily handle it, I had to let the relationship die when he withdrew from trying. So based on the present, I believed in faith for a long time that we would make a good long-term couple, and I continued to tell Beni this and spent time and emotional energy to continue the relationship as it presented itself. While I was away and ill, we both shared a common plan that I would return, he would move in with me, we would get to know each other better, and if things went well, we would one day marry.

Faith is not the plan; it is the belief about the quality of potential futures based on the known present. It is not a violation in this use to change one's mind and a change of faith. Faith is based on Truth, knowing who each of us is with strengths, weaknesses, abilities, and needs; and which events will likely face us are all truth and lead to faith, which gives a picture of the positive or negative things that may happen in our relationship. However, no amount of Truth can fully foretell the future. One must simply look at the facts and make decisions based on what one does know and weigh the likelihood of success based on our own truth, truth of our intended partner, and the amount of knowledge we have. But that is not a guarantee of happiness or successful arrival at an intended destination. Truth does not grant wishes. Truth is based on signs and experience, but faith, based on truth, is required to make a leap over a chasm of the unknown, whether that unknown is the next date or a future life together.

About a year ago, I met a guy who asked me in effect to wait for him as he worked out how to come out to his family. He had many wonderful traits, but I had no similar faith that we would be a good couple long term or even to be sure of the quality of our next date, so I was less willing to wait and told him so as the waiting dragged on and on. We do not know where Truth will lead. I probably could have summoned the mental will to marry Beni despite my misgivings, but that would have trampled my own truth and replaced faith with blind denial. The ability to persevere through strength of belief is not what I mean by faith, although that is often implied in traditional religion. I mean faith simply as an extrapolation inferred about the future based on current facts. In fairness, traditional religion also infers this as part of faith, but that is the only part I want to capture in this concept.

Traditional believers in Truth exhibit two difficulties in doctrine about faith that is inflexible. Martyrs are praised for faith from which they did not waver, even as it led the believer to their death. Please don't die for the partner of your dreams. Faith in this case is not an inflexible doctrine, but merely a prediction made based on visible facts. It's like playing in the stock market: select stock based on good information, having faith in an increase, but if circumstances change or new information comes to light, it may be time to reconsider the original choice in stocks, as well as a potential opportunity to buy others. Traditionally, there is sometimes an explicit or implicit expectation that correct belief will help make the dreams come true, sort of like a reward from a higher power. But the future cannot be controlled in this way. When it's time to choose, make the best choice on available information, but if things change, try your best to cut your losses and make another choice.

However, in contrast and complement to this principle, the present and the future can be controlled in circumstances we control. Then what we choose to believe in our own private truth we can control many of our outcomes our destiny. But traditionalists sometimes dismiss this power as self-delusion. A focus on the higher power can obscure the mechanism that the expectation itself affects the future. There are several areas I learned this in: First, as a teacher, I saw this effect when I expected students to be difficult. They usually were, or if I expected good behavior, it usually happened. I don't quite understand if my belief in the students transferred to their belief about themselves or if they responded to cues in the classroom management I designed as a result of my belief, but it was pretty consistent. The other area is in self-belief. to give extra effort or focus. Sometimes in exercise, for example, to believe that I can do the task greatly increases my endurance, or in a presentation, to believe that I would wow the audience often results in a self-confidence, which actually did move listeners greatly. Expectations and belief have a great deal of power, but they do not impact events far from ourselves. All humans have the ability to deny the facts and believe in something they simply wish were true, so we must continue cautiously so as not to simply clap our hands if we believe in fairies. Identification of truth is a product of both thought and feelings.

Truth Engineering

However, our choices of what to believe can strongly affect the world immediately near ourselves. I dated a man who on one date broke out into a torrent of human relations textbook trivia. I could have seen him as competitive or nerdy, but I chose to see it as an attempt to connect with me through something I had just mentioned. I once told Luis that our relationship would outlast the corona virus, which threatened our planned reunion by cancelling flights. Of course, this belief did not give us extra immunity, but belief in this statement strengthened us to push aside potential obstacles and not take a "no" very seriously, and it strengthened us to endure the wait to see each other again. To say things like that out loud creates a strange effect that makes them feel true, and we react accordingly. So in effect, I created my own truth. That is the truth I have now, but remember, personal truth can change, or one part become more important than another. In complete contrast to the old epistemology, I'm in charge of creating and maintaining my own Truth.

I think there is such thing as magic words. Those things that are not yet true can become true for us by speaking them out loud. So faith helps us make choices about next steps, priorities, and which truths to investigate further or create for ourselves or to pull from our gardens when they prove to be untrue.

Because the truth we believe in is strengthened by our belief, I have always disliked the unity candle ceremony that became popular at US weddings in the eighties, where each partner took up a candle to represent themselves, lit a central candle, and then blew out their own. The idea disturbed me that the individual no longer mattered in the union as well as the symbolism that there is now less light in the world because of the union rather than more, all in the name of a simple, unflinching unity. That is not the truth I want to create in my relationship. I expect and hope that when I do marry, we will continue to let our individual Truths shine and grow as we build new and wonderful parts to our mutual relationship, increasing our combined light in the world. Sometimes we'll need to make adjustments for each other without discussion, but I want to create truth that the union will be brighter than being two individuals.

Hope Is Rough

Once we have created a truth or faith, at the same time, hope is also created if the faith predicts something positive. Hope is kind of a byproduct, and in most cases, we do not intend to create hope, but hope is different than faith because it's not based on any evidence but mostly on what we would like to see happen. Hope has a great press agent, but in reality, it has a very low truth content, so hope is free to act like a cruel bitch (I mean that in the unisex way gay men use the word *bitch*). During my illness, away from Beni, I learned in fact how vicious hope can be. First, it kicked Beni's butt. Each time he hoped I would return and that the separation was almost over, reality would slam him against the wall, knocking the wind out of him. Then hope would mock him. Then, most insidious of all, hope co-opted me to draw him back in for another round. Then when Beni had no more will left to hope, he withdrew from me, which hurt incredibly. I wished for many months that he would change and really see me and really love me. In that disappointment, hope kicked my butt too. From this, I learned to guard against some kinds of hope. In the same way, I hoped that Beni would be my life partner, but my hope was built on some false assumptions, so I had to abandon them at great personal pain.

As I left Germany for the final time, it was tempting to make myself feel better by creating hope around future scenarios. It felt good to imagine myself returning to Germany as head of our office in Berlin or holding a partner's hand the next time I had to walk through the Stuttgart airport. But those victory scenarios were far too restrictive to be realistic or helpful in the longer term. What if I have a partner who feels uncomfortable holding hands in public or if we have to run to the gate and so can't hold hands? Is the whole day ruined then? I tried to be deliberately careful which hope I created for myself, in case, I have to wrestle with later. Instead, I focused on faith that I had done the right thing in coming back to Germany to sort out my head and my life, and in the faith that I'm a quality man who can attract a quality partner and faith that I have the talent and connections to continue to do well at work, whether that takes me to Berlin or elsewhere. Wouldn't that be pathetic to see me moping after being assigned to London or Sydney because I didn't get Berlin? We must be careful about the hope we create, or it may come back to bite us. Growing your own truth allows the grower to be selective, but we need to use that freedom wisely, and remember that hope is not Truth.

As an analogy, hope is like a heavy load that must be carried, so be sure of the destination. Recently, I went on an errand to have a lock opened on a small safe to which I had lost the key. I'd visited the lock shop and been assured they could do the work, so I tried to carry the twenty-pound safe to the shop. That's faith that they could do the work. I got a bit lost on the way but kept trying to find the shop. I would think I had a clever directional insight for a moment and carry the safe a block or two further, but then learned I was wrong and had to carry it back the way I had come. Getting to the shop was my hope, mixed in with some knowledge and experience (faith) of the actual location. Hope is like that safe—it's difficult to just abandon because it's the point of the mission, but one must carry it around while trying to figure things out. It's easy and natural to continue to encourage oneself by thinking that you're almost there and just a little bit more and you'll have it, but a realistic look at how much more is required can sometimes be enough to make us drop the safe and abandon the mission or try a radically different approach. Don't try to manage more hope than you can handle if it turns heavy or vicious.

I think I learned hope more from the rhythm of my family life as a child, rather than through religious instruction. As a child, the family had regular good times interspersed with long periods of boredom and hard work. To get between the good times, I learned to hope and look forward to the next good thing—looking forward to Christmas or a visit from my mom or even hoping for a good lunch while working in the yard.

And we can't live without hope; by definition, that will make us hopeless. So sometimes hope can become vicious and cruel, as well as others, when it is reassuring and strengthening. In the first instance, hope is more uncontrolled and burly than the other. Hope with a limited lifespan seems a good bet, which can be very useful, but never have time to turn on me. Hope is essential at the beginning of a relationship, as we take risks and invest effort, time, and love. Or hope can also be very useful to get through relational difficulties or conflicts. As I took risks in meeting new people, the hope that a group or individual looked promising helped me relax, get through the nervousness, and overcome the desire to just stay home. This kind of short-span hope is often quickly rewarded with positive feedback, or to go back to the beginning, the hope of a better relationship leads us to do otherwise frightening things like outing ourselves and sharing our truth with others. We empower hope but then have little control over how our hope will use its power.

In waiting to reunite with Luis after the coronavirus, I have learned from my mistakes of waiting to see Beni. Luis originally planned in May to come to the US, but flights stopped until April and May looked unlikely. Being out of work also sapped his money so to re-group and to have a better time together, he suggested waiting until August to come see me. I felt and said I might go crazy if I have to wait until August and briefly planed to go to Ecuador in June or July if flights are working by then. I had initially bent all my hopes around May, but realized I could be setting myself up for a large disappointment, so we talked tentatively and imagined our reunion in a multitude of flavors and times and places. This gives more joy in imagining more widely as well as protecting us from being hurt or exhausted by false, overly specific hope. We have allowed ourselves to dream freely about a Christmas together since that seems far enough away to be safe and since my daughters will be with their mother this year. In the meantime, that has somehow refocused us on the present, and with our emphasis there, we find new excitement and surprise daily in loving each other rqther than simply waiting on the future.

One night, I couldn't sleep and got up to work. I wrote Luis an e-mail at 4:00 a.m. to describe an idea I had and told him that I had to share it with the man I consider my life partner. He was thrilled to read it when he finally got up and showered me in return with a description of the time he first first got up the courage to introduce himself to me in Ecuador. I had never heard so much of the story before and felt honored and loved by the feelings and his willingness to share them.

We are not yet married, but our commitment to each other grows daily in lieu of focusing on a future hope. We receive daily presents we create for each other, like my early morning e-mail and his self-disclosure.

Hallelujah, It's Raining Men!

I originally conceived of this book as a "how to find the man of your dreams." But while my writing occasionally takes on that tone, I'm glad I didn't take that approach because in the end, my best and most wonderful prospects for a long-term relationship didn't come through careful hoping, planning, or method but by being in the right place at the right time. I met Luis because I happened to meet a friend in the street as I was wandering lost one day in Ecuador. Luis was a friend of this guy and later asked him for an introduction to "that gringo." Luis saw me and fell for me that day by chance. As we started exchanging messages, alarm bells went off that what I was doing felt wrong because of my relationship with my current boyfriend, but the mutual attraction was strong and undeniable, so I explored it further, setting myself the limit to not have sex with Luis. I didn't, but our attraction only grew, and I had never experienced anything like it. I could think of many reasons why we were a good match, even a better match than my boyfriend at the time, but I was haunted by questions if it is somehow tainted or wrong. I decided to just wait and see what happens, but the point remains that this strong connection happened through no effort of my own.

Surprising as well, my company agreed to let me go overseas again, and when I arrived in Ecuador, I learned how difficult it is to find a boyfriend there. I went dancing with gay friends several times, frankly hoping to find a new direction to move into, but it became clear that most Ecuadorian gay men were consumed with keeping up an appearance of being straight, and several guys who had caught my attention spent the night dancing with women. I was the only one on the dance floor who was actually "out." I felt embarrassed, lost, and lonely.

It was by complete chance that I met Beni on a night we happened to be in the same bar. In a final example, about two years ago, I had been feeling rather low and realized I needed to reconnect with my spiritual side, even unsure what that meant. A wild man I met in the sauna and dated a few times suggested an LGBTQ-affirming church in the middle of town, which I mentioned earlier, so I decided to try it out to see what happened, moving forward in hope and part in faith. I did not expect what came next. I felt a little odd hoping and even praying to meet a man at church, but that was a wonderful secondary goal, and I noticed several cute men during the service. Unfortunately, most of them moved to sit with their partners, and there were about five gay couples in the congregation. I had a harder time picking out the lesbian couples because black women are so demonstrative with each other, I couldn't sort the romantic couples from the good friends.

The church happened to be having a celebration that Sunday with a potluck afterward. After the service, as the congregation rearranged the meeting space and brought out tables, I scanned the room, wondering where I should sit. My eyes landed on a cute, flamboyantly dressed Latino whose status seemed high enough that other gay men would likely sit by him. There was an open seat available across from him, and I took it, with no more than polite church talk and a brief introduction. As people continued to find their seats, I struck up a conversation with this wonderful Latino named Antonio. I really admired his jewelry, and as I talked about his rings, I learned one dating tip worth sharing: talking about a man's rings is a wonderful flirtation device because it gives an excuse to hold his hand. So here, I was talking, flirting, and holding hands with a cute man in church. Violation of the expectations of my religious upbringing continued that day and still mess with my head.

It felt somehow inappropriate flirting in church, and talking about sex felt awkward at a later meeting when we got that far. At that first encounter, we went to get food together. He said he was getting a divorce from his husband, and I shared that I was in the process as well from my wife. He then said, "I'm available." We talked and held hands for quite a while that day until we finally decided to slowly walk to the subway together. I invited him to dinner for later in the week, and we dated for about six months. We were so well matched I realized that no level of planning could have organized it, and given where we met, it's hard not to wonder about divine intervention.

I have very little advice on dating except to implore the reader to get out there and meet many people and stay close to your truth. When the time is right to meet that wonderful someone, it will happen. This book is about how to build your truth, so when the time comes, you can recognize that person and be well prepared to share yourself with him or her and have skills to graciously understand your new friend's truth as you grow together. That's what Antonio and I did for six months, growing together, and my truth felt so validated, and the connection felt so right. And I can still say that it was right, even with the knowledge that the relationship didn't work out in the long term.

With Great Power Comes Great Caution

The search for truth is fun and exciting, but sometimes truth itself is not. Sometimes truth is disappointing, like learning that Beni and I were not as right for each other as I had dreamed or Antonio's truth that he was not interested to go overseas with me. Truth should not be judged by its fun or excitement factor because sometimes even the best truth is beautiful simply because it's true, like a real connection with another person that's consistent and ongoing. I think that's why sex can be so confusing; it's often very fun and exciting while sometimes revealing relatively little of truth. It can be very true, and feelings around this important activity should not be ignored, but its direction is often unclear, with quick highs and little real evidence of depth or endurance. I believe there is such a thing as revealed truth, which can come to us through wise people or important texts. These can give us clues where to find truth. However, we should not allow these types of revealed truths to trample other truth in our lives or those of other people.

Almost the End

I did eventually find a way to date in Ecuador, dated several men, and eventually lived with a gorgeous younger man, named Rene, who perhaps distorted my objectivity. As I faced an uncertain future, I originally had faith it would be a good relationship, based on evidence of the good times we had together. My relationship with Rene was very different than with any previous man, but he seemed a good fit for me. Our center of connection was not going out or sex but verbal banter and play, like childhood friends. Our life seemed one big problem-solving puzzle as we regularly disagreed, but there was an ineffable spark between us that I had not experienced before and which contained lots of daily joy. I learned to love Rene in a way that I only suspected existed. My inner child, who loves Mary Poppins and Arthurian legends, seemed to love and find many accommodations for his inner child who preferred *Power Rangers* and *Transformers*. At one point, I raised the issue that I felt unhappy in our sex life, and it took a great deal of faith and hope for me to fully open up that truth to him. In fact, he ranted and complained about my comments for several weeks, but I believed in my truth enough to persevere. I also created a truth that I felt in my soul, and by stating it out loud, it become concrete and very true.

Early in our relationship, I had difficulties in changing my habit of chasing multiple men. I explained to Rene that good sex with him could keep me absolutely faithful, and in fact, I used visualizations of sex with Rene to throw other fantasies under the bus. It proved to be very true, but he did not understand my need of him. Rene became my new standard, as I deliberately and willfully created the truth that

Rene was all I needed, but I eventually saw that I was wrong and needed more than he could give; I felt flattered that this handsome young man wanted to live with me and so I put up with far too much crap. I felt confident, beyond being hopeful every day. I didn't just hope that he would come back to live with me each night, I had the confidence of many nights to know that he would. Occasionally, it struck me how much faith and hope I was putting in this man and how much he had chosen to invest in me, and it struck me as odd that when Kae came to visit that the two of them could not find ways to be friends, so I continued to question. In short, I continued to walk down a street where there was a rational chance I could be mugged or hit by a car, but there was also a rational chance that I would not be and might find something glorious at the end of the street, so I kept walking. I kept an eye open to increase my chances of survival and tried to avoid the alleys that had less light. As that relationship began to fall apart and it was clear Rene was avoiding time with me and unwilling to work out disagreements except to insist that I shut up. I met Luis out of the blue and my truth resonated with his beyond lust, beyond hope, and beyond my imagination.

Chapter 9

Weeding the Truth Garden

What if I'm wrong?

So how or should one maintain belief in one's truth when this truth may turn out to be wrong? And when is it time to ditch the heavy weight in the nearby bushes? Does this negate the idea of personal truth? This is certainly not a question unique to gay relationships, and I don't believe my answer is terribly unique either. No, but it means we must be realistic and have a sense of perspective. After many doubts and arguments, I came to believe in both our potential for long-term fidelity to each other. It's similar to the way I used to maintain religious belief, which at the time was like growing my own truth that sometimes faltered in its personal applications, and although it looked very much like the truth of other believers, the truth was of my own choosing.

As a religious example, in response to the commandment to love my neighbor as myself, I would often show kindness to strangers or people who were not kind in return because I believed that God had given me an opportunity to show love to someone in need. My specific application to a particular individual sometimes proved incorrect, and I was occasionally cheated or taken advantage of, so I pulled that particular application from my Truth and did not allow myself to be further disadvantaged by that individual. However, that did not diminish the truth or the general principle, but circumstances needed adjustment. A romantic relationship is the same, and an individual simply holds a belief as true until it is known to be untrue, investing more power in the truth as it proves its worth. There is no penalty for the previous error unless we are completely dependent on that perceived application, but simply an ongoing good-will attempt to maintain truth as judged by the individual. In intimate relationships, it feels a bit unfaithful to hold any doubt, but as rational persons, we must allow for possibility that we could be wrong, and as living beings, we continue with what we believe to be true. So as Rene's partner, I knew that he sometimes made up excuses to dodge out of staying home with me in order to hang out with friends. Initially, I felt very threatened, as I didn't know if these friends were dates or who they were. But I came to learn a fuller picture, realized he needed that time away, and I didn't feel threatened by this blip in his general dedication to me, although I did want more of his time and asked for it regularly.

In my relationship with Beni, I made choices based on what I believed the world to be. We did not get as far as actual marriage, that would have been truly too late to discover my misperception, but I felt satisfied with the process. I fought and struggled to get back to Stuttgart because I believed we could have a great relationship, and I had enough time to see from Beni that I was wrong and that the relationship would not have fit my truth without some further adjustments. I tried one more time to find a way we could spend time together and evaluate possibilities, but when that proved impossible, I identified my bottom line and pulled the plug when it was not met. It was very much worth my struggle to evaluate this relationship because it lent me an opening to dispel the myth I had created that Beni was the only possible man for me. In the same way, I was content to move on with the peace of mind that Rene had many desirable traits and many shortcomings, but more powerful forces move our stars, and in the same way, I learned in the end that Rene and I could not be the couple I had perceived.

Again in Ecuador, health issues arose, and I had to return to the United States. I felt extremely stressed, as I tried to wrap up my work and deal financially with the sudden change. At the same time, I was reminded that Rene had little capacity for empathy. One night, I was exhausted after a day of work and stress, got home, and fell asleep on the sofa. When Rene came home, he woke me with indignity, asking where dinner was that I had previously offered to make. He then pushed to get it quickly, and when I brought it, he complained that the dinner was not anything special. This one incident didn't cause our break up, but it reminded me of the many other instances of his lack of empathy: how he avoided discussing sex with me, avoided Kae, dodged communicating with me about his return from time with friends or his future plans with them, and his complete inability to listen or understand the kind of stress I was undergoing in this sudden departure. The plan had been for me to petition for him to come to the US on a fiancé visa, where we would be married after waiting four months to a year for the visa. I didn't readily have money for the petition and knew I would have a terrible time waiting for Rene to arrive, and I realized the inconsiderate treatment I was getting was not worth all the work and worry I was required to put into the relationship. I first told Rene that things needed to change, and then when he complained that he could not help me, I told him the plan was cancelled and that he would not be joining me. I was not sure if his denial of these statements was a tactic to avoid compliance or a further example of his in ability to listen and empathize. But I had had enough of carrying the whole relationship on my back, returned to the US alone again, and spent the next several months re-explaining to Rene my decision, which he had not processed.

That was the most troublesome breakup I have ever endured, as we both had become used to the idea that we had found our life partner and could easily fall into the patterns of our banter and expression of care. Perhaps it would have all been fine, but I had no more faith in Rene as he had failed at empathy and refused to listen to me time and time again. I cannot deny that my need to be treated better by a partner, especially one for whom I was to give so much, was crucial and non-negotiable.

I believed the same with Beni as in faith, I tried my best to get back to Stuttgart. The fact that we had tremendous arguments as we restarted did not invalidate my faith. I moved forward based on the best information I had. Nor did it mean that my perception was not true. For me, it was absolutely true until the moment I realized it wasn't. With both Beni and Rene, I think I can say that my perception was true at one moment in time, and when I later found it false, I trimmed it way back, what turned out to be a falsehood growing in my truth garden. My return to Stuttgart, in fact, led me to see that Beni and I had some areas we would need to resolve in order to be truly good for each other, and problems with Rene highlighted a huge flaw I had ignored. So I made some adjustments in my Truth. I then took the truth of what I needed but was not getting and begin to press it home with each. I needed to have these issues met, but both Beni and Rene came to a point where they balked and told me he had had enough and that I was just a bad man. However, I could not disregard my truth. There were still people who believed me a bad person for coming out as gay and divorcing my wife, but in all these instances, I realized that I couldn't make everyone happy on my own and abandoned the effort, ditching the hope of the life I expected in the bushes rather than carry it any more. Both my arms and my heart felt lighter for the relief. This reaction is normal and natural, especially as two people are reflecting on and reacting to the same set of facts.

So, reader, are you tired yet of each additional twist to the plot on the way to a hopefully happy ending? Well, let me tell you that I am exhausted by this point as well. I suppose that exhaustion with the process is best combatted with a faith that things will come out OK in the end. Let me assure you that things did come out very well but ask you to keep in mind that, at that point, I was beginning to lose hope of finding my happy ending.

Garden Timing

An actual garden as well as a truth garden is always about the precise moment of use—when the vegetables are ripe or the flowers in bloom. This doesn't change the truth of being or disqualify the plants from being useful in the future. Most people leave a good blooming flower in the ground even if it's not blooming at the moment. However, as one manages a garden, a frequent task is to pull out the things that have been expended or are no longer valuable, like deadheading flowers, as well as planting new things for the future. The same is true of a truth garden. Personal Truth is sometimes only valid in the moment, and we must monitor the garden and pull out the things that are dead or no longer useful because they take up space and are useless. We must also see where and when there is space to grow something new. I will enumerate the several types of things that seem true, and in some senses are, but are hindrances because they do not reflect or help with the present:

1. As mentioned previously, proposed solutions are not truth and must not be treated as enduring truth. The truth is the goal that the proposed solution would fill, such as "I would like you to pay more attention to me." That is useful (and a very good *I* statement). To say "I want you to respond to my texts as soon as I send them" is neither truth nor helpful because it is an absolute demand with no room for the needs of the listener. Solution ideas should not be treated as truth.

2. Sometimes truth expires and is no longer true. For example, I had a very strong need to return to Stuttgart to see friends and close out my existence there. To some degree, I still feel that need. I also feel a strong need to take a boyfriend to the CSD festival in Köln so that I can be one of those guys reveling in his freedom. While I feel both these things strongly, I realize they may no longer be important enough to me to count as truth in my future, and I need to weigh any

costs of achieving them carefully based on their real, current value to me at the time.

3. Finally, we may need to question the importance of something I call nostalgic truth, things which are true based on something in the past but may no longer be as important as it once was or may have taken a useful form only in a different time frame. For example, often adults who felt they received too little attention from their parents feel an imperative to spend large amounts of time with their own children as a way to make up for the past hurt that was caused them. This can be a noble act of learning from the past, but the adult needs to evaluate if it is still true for him/her and if the time and effort is worth the actual payoff. Is it worth forcing the children to spend family time hiking while they are griping and crying? I also find myself often attracted to men who remind me of the cool kids in my adolescence. That perspective represents little of my current truth, and while I may be attracted as I was to Rene, I must be cautious how far I let such relationships run. While the need may feel very right to the once injured adult, or now lonely adult, this may be a false kind of nostalgic truth in the present if the adult no longer has that need in the present or if the accompanying solution is more trouble than it's worth. Someone who experienced poverty in the past may feel a need to obsessively earn money to keep that past pain away. That truth should be evaluated in the light of other truths and other personal goals.

So if truth can be reworked and engineered, won't it be easier to change my truth that I am gay? Or simply stifle the need to be with a man? No. Personal truth cannot and should not be bent to match society's or someone else's truth. Sexual orientation is a special area that is so personal that it is an especially inviolable area in which to try to change that truth. As a recent protest sign in Australia read, "I can no more choose to be gay than I can choose to be a unicorn." Some things are just not possible. If the space for personal truth is surrendered to others or to society, the individual is on the verge of being lost. Furthermore, I use the word *truth* because it is so much more than preference or whimsy. A personal truth at least feel inalterable. I suggest there that sometimes it can be changed or selected, but the central idea remains that it is fundamentally unalterable. I am suggesting here the need to monitor one's own truth, not to transform it for the sake of someone else but to maintain the quality of one's own garden. It's counterproductive to treat something untrue as though it were genuine and important. Priorities get unbalanced, and the individual can become disoriented.

And Love

In my return to Stuttgart, I learned the importance of love more than anything else. Love is different from Truth and in no way is it a derivative. It is a range of emotional responses, expressions, and actions that support another person and grow the relationship between them, often in a place where the truths held by two people do not match. My truth and faith seemed to say that Beni and I would be perfect together, but I didn't experience enough love from him to bridge remaining differences. His truth said that work was most important, while my truth focused on the spontaneous and emotional; love is the bridge that could have made these differences work together and cover the rough patches between them. I used to blurt out that I love a man when something he did or is doing delights me and I overflow with emotion, but love shows itself best when the partner begins to seem less appealing. Love is what binds two people into a relationship and makes any remaining differences manageable.

In our final breakup, Beni told me that he had tolerated all my issues and problems, but that is far short of love. Love notices the less than ideal and even the hurtful and finds a way to keep it from getting in the way. Beni tried to meet me for fun at odd hours, as he was available. That was love, as he sought to meet my need through extra effort. Similarly, I suggested that I take over all the shopping and cooking for the two of us to save him time for more work and rest while I gained the guaranteed time of eating together. I had no particular need to cook and shop for him, and I had no illusion but that I would be paying for groceries. I didn't know why he dismissed that idea, as he did many of the kindnesses I tried to show him to patch over our differences. Perhaps he felt a loss of control or that it somehow meant he needed to show me more. I will never know. I can truly and objectively say that Rene and I loved each other because we found ways to cover many gaps when we fell short of meeting each other's needs in some ways, But the final gap proved too big, and while still in Ecuador, I tried to give Rene many opportunities to help bridge that gap, but he did not take any of them. If it is all mine to manage, I cannot. Love is not one way or one partner always giving in or becoming a doormat. Our truths remain true, and I continued to try to understand his truth and explain mine to Rene as many times as necessary.

Personal truth needs care and attention in order to thrive and grow. It needs inputs of time and materials to produce, but it is so worth the effort to share and work together with others to share ideas, harvest the crop, share techniques, and reduce the need for mass-produced vegetables. The team effort is especially important in developing a relationship. Truth needs friendships and partnerships to keep the gardener strong and to give a second perspective.

In the end, having is not the goal of life, even having a wonderful relationship or an amazing crop of truth. The important thing in life is connecting. I believe that I have reached my happy ending, which I will describe shortly, but things can happen to that ending. One of us could die early, or some disaster can happen between us; but I have faith that Luis will be a wonderful life partner, so I keep faithful to him and continue to express and develop love and support for my partner. Truth has no hold on fate. I could have died from recent medical issues several times now. My truth cannot protect me from such things. I've been on a long journey that connected me with many men, but each connection was valuable even after I am making a life with someone else. For example, I note that I need to be quite emotional at times, so I need someone flexible and passionate, and because I know myself and my truth, those issues quickly rose in my new relationship with Luis. My need was quickly addressed initially because I knew what I need and because he listens and loves me. He has had less relational experience than me, and so I notice that he raises fewer issues than I do. I also note he is sometimes a workaholic, so I have volunteered to take the role of urging him to rest and connect and offered to be our social planner. He appreciates the care and accepted. He sees me stressing and sometimes tells me how I'm feeling before I mention it and often suggests a course of self-care. Good partners should help strengthen each other's truth and know each other's truth in order to best help and protect the partner.

I am learning this truth as I wait for Luis to join me in the US and live with me. We agreed that we need more time together to get to know each other before an ultimate commitment, so during his already planned vacation to the US, he will be spending less time with his friends and more time with me, and I have been invited to accompany him to meet these friends. However, the outbreak of the coronavirus has put his vacation plans on indefinite hold, and waiting is excruciating, as I realize I am mostly hoping rather than knowing that all will be fine simply because we lack experience together and I have had less time to gather Truth. As we text each other nearly constantly, I do realize that how truly empathetic he is, sometimes telling me what mood I am in based only on his experience with me or a bit of tone he picks up. In his disappointment of dealing with the setback and fear of losing his job, I see real truth of his comfort and ability to handle his own emotion and mine. These are truths and give me hope that we will be a great couple. We also continue to find things we have in common and see some of our desires for a reunion and a happy relationship are very much in sync. He thrills me just being who he is and reports a similar feeling about me. I have to be honest with myself despite attendant fear that it is possible I can be wrong about Luis, but I don't think so, and we continue to move forward and bond ourselves tightly together, giving hope a great deal of latitude, but trying to give ourselves safe distance if something goes wrong. This will not guarantee a happy ending, but it seems logical based on the known and it does feel comforting while sitting at home alone. I keep the hope as light as I can but at the same time cling closely to it. I watch my situation to recognize safety valves if things do not go as expected, but still I hope and plan around a happy reunion.

Protecting Your Truth

Like any garden, personal truth is constantly under attack, and care must be taken to prevent damage. I'll start by discussing my previous, sense of self-care to contrast some key elements that are actually harmful. And since this book is written for those with a past in normative, absolute truth, this word of caution is important. Part of the religious instruction I received included ways to protect myself, which really boiled down to protecting the indoctrination I had taken in. Things that were fun were always to be held as suspect and examined for traps and tricks. Unique things were suspect as well. An idealized sense of what my truth should look like was the guide, and self-care was basically designed to maintain conformity. Creating theater for church frequently crossed that line, and I observed a great deal about the mechanisms of conformity and personal truth. I stirred a good deal of controversy one year when I wrote a Christmas play about a family in which one child character told his sister to shut up. One night backstage, the cast was abuzz about this phrasing. Some held that it was a poor example to be presented in church, while others liked it because "that's how my kids talk to each other. I don't know about yours." There was a regular measure of conformity expected of others and the self, which was often termed as some sort of self-care. This is not what I mean. Protecting your own truth does not mean policing one's self to meet a certain norm. That is exactly not the point of growing one's own truth, but a garden needs to be protected from opportunistic pests like birds and slugs and neighborhood kids who may steal the flowers or fruit. And I always need to take care that I do not damage my garden myself by stepping on young sprouts or accidently pulling up a good plant, thinking it's a weed.

Sometimes I find myself wishing for the past kind of conformity in order to be more in sync with others or to have a clear plan to follow, so I think about trimming my truth so it looks like that of others. That would be a terrible mistake. Every truth must grow to its own potential, and if a plant is no longer pleasing or productive, then it should be pulled on its own lack of merit, not prematurely trimmed for superficial, aesthetic reasons. Sometimes I've found myself trying to fit my relationship with men into the heteronormative molds I learned as a child and practiced while married. I talk about the dog like he's our child and start relating to other couples through dinner parties and set-piece social gatherings. These are not bad things, but I have to be careful not to let the form dictate the content. If dinner parties are no longer fun, I need to be free to let them go. Truth is a living thing that continues to change and grow, and it must be allowed these privileges. As I plan for my current relationship, there are many variables and options in play and I may need to make hard choice between them in the future based on my truth. That's why I abandoned the original construction metaphor of this book. Truth, is much more flexible, organic, and multifaceted than a building site. Building also implies a clear plan ahead of time. Truth is full of surprises. Sometimes being a gay couple points out the absurdity of trying to conform to societal expectations such as opening doors for each other, which really depends on who is walking faster on a particular day and neither of us cares. We always have the option to change our mind or grow something new, so connection with others rather than submitting to norms keeps our own truth fresh and vibrant.

Communication is unique between different people and must be adapted to the personalities and situation. While Luis is still in Ecuador, we are finding ways to connect to each other even if it comes through understanding the difference in meaning to the other guy between a voice mail and a text or to understand when an immediate response is needed or when more thought in response is better. These nuances take time but are very much worth it.

The world needs more respect for one another's differences, and it starts with self-respect. You must respect your own truth based on who you are as an individual to have faith that that it will produce a good crop and is worth the water and care and the courage to make changes as needed, whether that courage involves facing a truth yourself or sharing it with others.

Even more destructive to my truth than false hopes or even deliberate maliciousness of others is the harshness I occasionally unleash on myself. I recently noticed that some of my usual comforts and turn-ons are just no longer working, and I can hear a voice in my head, scolding, "See? You're not really gay. Things never work out for perverts!" Or sometimes, past rejections quickly turned into self-recriminations. In the old worldview, that voice would be called the devil, and I think that concept is valuable here around personal truth as well, kind of a self-inflicted accusation that comes up when things don't go as expected. We need to protect ourselves from that kind of self-criticism, whatever its name. The best solution to that kind of self-recrimination comes straight out of Sunday school. First, a thoughtful examination is needed to see if anything is actually wrong and, after that, a strong self-assurance of faith that you are on the right path or charting a correction. Next, that your own truth is valuable, and that you've made the right choices for things to turn out in the end until you can feel the peace to continue or have assurance in a new path. That kind of self-care is important to tend your truth with reverence and care and to respect yourself and your truth as it cross pollinates with a world of difference. That is self-care.

I've experienced depression previously in life, but nothing like the breakup with Beni, including a loss of hope. I questioned myself and everything I believed and even started to notice how easy it would be to just slide off the railing of my apartment balcony. Hope takes a heavy toll, and disappointed hope can be caustic. Caring for your truth is self-care, and self-care also involves connecting with a loving and caring family or network. For me, sharing the depth of my grief with my sister really helped me through the toughest periods, which was a more helpful conclusion than the need to keep hoping through difficulties, as I had been taught as a child. Hope is a difficult burden, and sometimes we need to allow ourselves to let it go. Hope is belief against the evidence where growing truth is about treating the evidence with the utmost respect. Faith is a certainty about the future based on current evidence. Hope is like insecticide in the garden; it's necessary, but it must be used with caution.

Chapter 10

Brass Tacks and Gold Rings

All this truth growing and connecting to others sounds good, but at least some readers must be asking "So what?" In this next section, I leave behind the theoretical, religious, and philosophical and even ease up on the romantic and talk about the practical implications of how important having my own healthy, strong truth was in the process of transitioning back to the US and creating a meaningful life for myself after I lost all that I had built in Stuttgart. I'm going to be practical, not that romance or sexual identity has to be practical, but to balance out the perspective.

In short, our own Truth guides and directs us to where we need to be and where we can be happiest and most productive when life is in flux and nothing is certain or unlimited possibilities present themselves for choice. I used to believe that endless choice was the ideal situation in life, but as I grow older and realize that I don't have unlimited time to try everything and learned that each attempt has many costs, I saw that a sense of direction is extremely valuable. Having a clear sense of truth serves as both a beacon and ballast for life's ship when the waters get rough and uncertain.

I'll discuss the application of these principles to my quest for a life partner shortly, but I first want to illustrate them in less complex areas to illustrate the principles themselves. First, knowing the truth of what one likes and does not like is an extremely helpful guide, especially when there are many choices. When I returned to company headquarters in the US, I was given a job to oversee and examine several new customer service initiatives. My instructions were fairly broad and a bit vague. I was expected to understand seven different new customer service improvement initiatives. All but one had someone else in charge of the actual initiative and doing the work, but I was to understand the state of each improvement, examine the connections between them, report back, and fix anything that needed doing. There were a few specific projects the boss had in mind, but my effort was mostly mine to commit. I have a passion to ensure that employees are treated well, and a common theme I noticed in these initiatives was that employees felt pushed, bruised, and resentful of the initiatives. One of the senior managers mocked the initiatives as a waste of time that would be better spent on employee discipline to ensure work got done in the "proper" manner. It was sort of the galley slave mentality that "beatings will continue until morale improves." So I had a different and new way of looking at the issue: how to engage employees in ensuring the success of the initiatives.

This is a necessary and important aspect of the process that had previously not been considered. I found it and found my place and my value added to the process because of my truth, steps that were extremely useful. How the initiatives ended or whether or not I was rewarded for my work is irrelevant. The point is that my truth gave me meaning and direction; it gave me a starting place to call my own to link my work together and motivate me through it. I continued to accumulate tasks and direction in that environment, but it was my truth that got me started. In past company tasks, my truth, truly lived, built huge amounts of personal capital from which I can draw to fuel future projects. My first real success in the company came when I worked in the office of one of the senior executives. Given my values, I encouraged rather than harangued employees to complete tasks, and the kindness was remembered. Years later, I continue to encounter employees who feel they are in my debt and will help with any project I request. One's own truth gives strength and quickly points in the right direction.

But truth is not only practical. We can also find our best comfort in our truth. My oldest daughter lived and attended college about one hundred miles outside of the city where I worked at headquarters, so she kindly offered to let me stay at her place when I first moved back. I would get up early and take the train into the city to look for apartments, work in the office, and take care of administrative details. I love my daughter and enjoyed living with her, but I realized quickly that I needed a place of my own to form a nexus for my new life in the new place. So I made it my focus and my passion to get into an apartment. After I identified one, I harassed the management company whenever the process slowed, and the apartment search gave me a place to focus my efforts and truly celebrate successes as they occurred. I would tell my entire circle of friends when I passed a significant milestone, and sensing my need, they celebrated with me. The apartment search and the victories along that path gave me some real comfort and direction in the initial days of my new life. And the truth created as I imagined myself in my own safe nest in an interesting part of town sustained me in that new life.

There were several times I pulled out truth to comfort myself. As I left Stuttgart, I wondered if I would ever have the kind of friends and experiences and life that I had built there. But then I focused on the truth that at one time I had no one and no friends and no direction in Stuttgart either, and I remembered those sad times shortly after my wife left for the US when I felt alone, but I tried new things and met new people and developed a wonderful life for myself in Stuttgart, so why couldn't I do it again? I began to do just that in the US, taking my own advice of how and where to find men, trying out and finding bars and restaurants I liked and finding groups in which to meet people. Attempts to recreate those feelings from Germany or depend on individual institutions were not always successful, but new institutions and opportunities filled their place. Gay pride celebrations in the US are nothing like the shrines of acceptance I found in Germany. I took a hotel in the city for a couple days during pride, but met no one and had no interesting experiences except to notice that pride feels a lot like St. Patrick's Day.

When every bar drapes itself in the prescribed colors, people gather their own set of friends before going to the bar, and there's no way for a single person to tell where to find an actual Irishman or where to find other interesting gay men. The US has other opportunities, however. Meet Up, the online group gatherer, is wonderful to find new people and new places to meet new people. I was nervous before my first group meeting, like going to CSD by myself. It felt awkward, but it turned out fine, and while some groups felt more inclusive and supportive than others, I found several groups and multiple individuals who filled up my emotional needs. That's the kind of truth I pulled out to encourage myself.

My memories of success and truth felt like reservoirs of comfort and encouraging action plans for me in my new life. Americans are also very good at engaging strangers for no particular purpose. It was so hot one night that I took my shoes off to walk the last five blocks from the subway. A handsome young man came beside me and started talking about how comfortable I looked, and he told me he was on his way to work and therefore had to leave his shoes on and that it was his birthday. We talked pleasantly for several blocks until he soon left me for his job. America is unique for such random interactions. They don't feel very reliable because you can't just go find one. However, the sunshine they drop into life is priceless. The encounter was so wonderful, I thought about kissing the guy, but that's not a usual part of the American style of sharing, and I looked for him around the neighborhood for some time. The encounter had value at the moment, even though it was never repeated. It's important to remember that people who are not necessarily dates can fill many emotional needs in a sometimes lonely life. When I had no partner, I liked going to a restaurant or bar with a good vibe and just inhaling the milk of human kindness that swirls around. There's usually someone to interact with, whether I start the conversation or if they do.

Personal truth is a great way to start those conversations. I met lots of people walking around the neighborhood with my dog, and he started many conversations, as he is greeted by the other dogs.

Fortunately, the humans don't sniff one another's butts, but the process is much the same. I swear! One guy regularly flirted with me, as he talked about how he wished his dog got along better with other dogs. This kind of living out loud in a public place is animated by personal truth of what is important and how we choose to treat one another. My father likes to start conversations based on the T-shirt or baseball cap of a stranger, but those lead to far too many sports conversations for my taste. I like to pick up on the small hints that people expose of who they are, like when I exposed my bare feet and the other guy felt comfortable to tell me his plans for the evening. I never started a relationship with the owner of the unfriendly dog, but in some instances, these random neighborhood encounters lead to some very good times. When I first arrived and had no ability to cook for myself, I found a bar and grill with a couple cute bartenders and went back several nights in a row. I was simply following my truth. One cute guy was particularly taken that I came back hoping to see him again. The third night, he invited me out to his smoke break and sat on my lap the whole time. He later hopped up on the bar in front of me and invited me to have my way with him right there. We started a short but very intense relationship that night. That doesn't always happen, but it can. Gays are everywhere, and many will very much like to have someone to love. Knowing that others may be as desperate as I am is sometimes comforting. The barman's hints weren't subtle, but learning my way around the office, I often made it a point to pick up on any reticence of others. For example, if I suggest passing a document to someone for review and a coworker suggests avoiding that person, I ask questions and learn a great deal about the speaker and the person we are talking about.

Another truth that I've used to my advantage is that I really like to express myself through cooking, so inviting new acquaintances over for food became easy, and in my small apartment, the bedroom is not far away. Several interpreted the offer of food strangely, and I had to clarify that I didn't feel like they needed feeding per se, but they accepted my gift of self and enjoyed my cooking. Again, my truth led me forward to an opportunity.

However, what one doesn't like is a very effective tool to move one forward to the timely end of some relationships. The bar employee was rather young, and as we tried to create a more steady relationship, he would neglect to tell me the whole story of what he had in mind for the evening or prove helpless to keep things from interfering with our time together. After a while, I had to tell him that I felt tired of being his leftover time filler and needed some more dedicated time.

In addition to the barman, I met several men who were wonderful. Like earlier encounters, I needed to use my truth to sort the possibilities and priorities to wisely expend my time and emotional energy. Most of my life, I lived by a fairly hetero ethic of only dating one person at a time. I learned in the big city, however, that gay men don't always play that way and learned the new rules to the game. The barman made very clear from about the second date that we were casually dating. I was not quite sure why he felt the need to emphasize that. He had lots of female friends but wasn't dating any other men as far as I knew. I think he might have experienced some very possessive men in his past. But interest in more than one man at once made it clear that I would need to make choices and prioritize. This is not intended as a brag and actually feels awkward to admit, but at one time, I had close to ten men on my cell phone and chat site combined who could have quickly turned into dates if our free time coincided.

So I transitioned to the world of casual dating in the big city. In this period, I didn't know where any relationship would land or what priority anyone would take for me or the other man, but I was willing to go along to see what happened, and I continued to learn and grow as I experienced new things. I also learned that it's important to regularly share my truth with those whom I was most interested in pursuing or they won't understand where I'm coming from or get confused, even apprehensive as they experienced me. I needed to keep them updated with my thinking and feelings. I had two guys I really liked tell me that I was moving too fast in the relationship because they didn't see the process of how I got from just meeting to realizing that I could live my life with that man. My process was as I described previously. I took the things I could see in the relationship and imagined them in a future together to see if it would work. So I could see the relationship had promise and began to prioritize it more heavily, unfortunately without discussion.

My father used to say that I shouldn't date anyone I don't want to marry, and I think I absorbed that old-time approach too well, although it doesn't fit well with casual dating. I think I would rephrase that adage to advise not spending time, money, and emotional energy on someone who doesn't share my values and world outlook. That's where one's truth becomes the litmus test for action.

So I found two men who seemed to be exactly what I want in a man, but while I created truth in my mind that those relationships could work long term and thought I was even collaboratively planning a future together with one of them. They made it clear that I was moving too fast, and one said he felt uncomfortable because I had more going on in my head than in the relationship. I needed to better share what was going on in my head. I had told him often how much I liked him, but those conversations were part of the problem. I needed to tell him my truth of the importance of a lasting companionship and my belief and rationale that seemed to me that we could be good together long term. Maybe that would have at least helped my emotional state make sense to him. I probably needed to listen better as well to hear the things he needed from me. In the end, he broke up with me because he couldn't get a handle on what I was about and didn't think I heard or respected him. Can't blame him for calling it off, although it made me sad to lose such a good man.

Loneliness Is Real and OK

In my new life in the US, my thinking on hope continued to develop. As mentioned several times, more than anything, I want to find a life partner whom I realize that I want to be both a best friend and sex god. I didn't come across men like that every day, unfortunately, so it was a tough balance sometimes between staying true to myself, not becoming discouraged, and dealing with the loneliness highlighted by this search. I like the Rudyard Kipling poem I came across in the US called "If," on this point, "If you can dream and not make dreams your master … Yours is the Earth and everything in it." I still dream deeply of having a partner with me long term, but too often, the men in my past were unavailable, unresponsive, or uninterested; but that does not mean that my dream is wrong or untrue. I take great comfort from the very fact that I continue to regularly meet men with whom I can potentially be happy to live my life with, speaking to their prevalence, so I can believe that someday I will find one who is available and interested in growing a relationship with me. In the meantime, I need to guard my heart that the disappointment in delay didn't make me bitter or cause me to compromise what I need. While a relationship coming quickly would have been nice, it's not a requirement of my truth. I started keeping an ice bucket where I put notes of pleasant interactions and things that happened during the day or week. When I feel particularly low, I take them out and remember how many wonderful things I had experienced. Truth and dreams matter, but I must manage them carefully in a complex world.

CHAPTER 11

Summary

Speaking Truth in a Relationship

Relationship is about speaking and listening, and if that's the main thing the reader takes from my experience, I am satisfied.

In talking about the need for me to better share within a relationship, I must be cautious not to make the issue all about me. The other men should also talk about how they're feeling so that I can correct misperceptions or understand when I'm crowding their space. At one point, one guy thought I was pressuring him for sex, and sharing that revelation helped clear the air. I know my relationship with Rene could have benefited if he said more of what he thought and felt. If we focus only on what we one-sidedly can do to improve a relationship, it leads to both arrogance and self-criticism, neither of which is helpful.

Growing a partnership or friendship around two different truths is the realm of the *I* statement, an interpersonal communication concept developed by Thomas Gordon in the 1960s, which refers to statements that an individual uses to share about the self. They come in many flavors: "I feel," "I need," "I want," "I don't like," etc. Really any truth sharing with a partner or with a friend needs to proceed this way, even with the more ethereal "I believe." But in a relationship, whether between friends or romantic partners, these statements must come quickly in order to express discomfort or joy, let the other catch up, dodge a perceived problem, and maintain synchronization. The *I* statement always focuses on the speaker rather than on the behavior of the listener, so it avoids accusatory or arguable statements. For example, "That [what you just said] was very disrespectful" accuses the speaker of acting inappropriately, and it is better to say, "I felt disrespected when you said that." The *I* statement is more effective because it is more objective. There can be argument if an action or statement is inherently disrespectful, but if a person says s/he feels disrespected, the other can't very well say, "No, you didn't."

I statements carry a great deal of important personal truth quickly, but stay neutral. The guy who thought I was moving too fast but didn't break up with me had it about right. I told him how wonderful I was beginning to think he was, and he said, "That feels like you're moving too fast." I didn't know quite what to make of that, but I let it go for a bit and then asked him later if he was expressing concern for me becoming hooked on him too quickly or if he was feeling uncomfortable. He said he was uncomfortable, and so I told him the good things I saw in him and how those fit well with me. Questions can help as well. I caution any new practitioner of *I* statements to focus on the purpose rather than the words. Teenaged students to whom I taught this concept often felt very clever when they came up with statements like telling someone "I feel you're taking too much time in the bathroom." The word *feel* does not erase the accusatory content or make the statement any more about the self. An actual *I* statement would be something like, "I feel rushed and bothered when I have less than fifteen minutes to use the bathroom in the morning." There is more discussion about *I* statements and procedures for effective sharing of truth in appendix 1.

A good relationship is full of lots of truth sharing and negotiation and comparing personal needs between two truths; and even more so, good sex takes a lot of communication to get in sync, but I have met people who refuse to talk about feelings with a partner. My former mother-in law believed in a kind of mythology where if two people are meant to be together, they just know what the other needs.

A kind of miracle is needed without the use of good *I* statements and truth sharing, but fortunately a little talking works like a miracle.

Your truth is true and deserves respect. However, respect does not mean making demands upon others but upon presenting your truth and listening to those we love. Managing personal truth takes more work than simply pulling out a cookie cutter, but sharing it in actions and expressions of giving and talking fully pulls the individual into the tapestry of the world around him or her and connects to other people. There has been a long history of using common received truth to unite and enforce unity in a group of people. But personal truth does not undermine this order of society. It actually enhances it if handled properly. Communication ties one individual to another and the individual to the group. We need more truth sharing, not conformity, in order to make a more peaceful and stable world. Private truth is not about shunning others but about embracing the other in each of us to connect and find something new. Since personal truth is personal, it cannot be imposed by someone else. That is the only limit to a focus on personal truth rather than larger received truth. No one from the top can get everyone in line. That is also precisely the problem with gay conversion therapy. It's someone else's idea of how an individual should live forced upon him or her by another person with whom the patient is not in personal relationship. Personal truth requires both parties to be on the same page about sharing and receiving truth.

Pattern Finding

Humans like finding patterns and things that work. That is what has made us successful as a species, such as "Oh, your food is much more tasty and easier to chew after you cook it on the fire. Please show me again, how you make that fire." I think that is also the same spirit that causes us to look for universal moral truth to imitate and hold ourselves and others to a standard rather than this unpredictable personal truth business. I can definitely acknowledge this urge and, in fact, continue to look for more universal truths among the things that I have learned. Let me finally close with what I think I have found, not as a reversal of the importance of personal truth but as an affirmation of it as an example to lead us toward the more universal truth. I believe I have found two touch points of universal truth in my connection with my boyfriend, Luis. I do not claim that my writing is divinely inspired, but it is what I have found, and I defer to the reader's judgment, based on your own experience. In the end, I learned how long truth formation takes and wrote about it above. That's called life.

Wrapping Up My Search

After leaving Ecuador, I have looked for an ethic, especially a sexual ethic to guide me, and I take my answer from the example of an exceptional man I met shortly before leaving Ecuador. Luis (his actual name in honor of him) attracted my attention, and I attracted his. A mutual friend introduced me to Luis after Luis caught sight of me and asked for the introduction just as my relationship with Rene happened to be quickly falling apart. At first, Luis was very hesitant to get to know me, knowing that I was still in a relationship with Rene, and definitively, sex with me was off limits for himself while I was still with Rene. But we did meet a couple times at a restaurant, had good conversation, and kissed passionately for short periods. He did not want to interfere with an established relationship. But once I called it off with Rene, I pursued Luis with vigor. I concluded from this experience that patience in relationships is rewarded. Also, it's true one wants what is set as off limits, and I became much more direct in my conversations with Luis, telling him that I wanted him as my partner in part because of his respect for my previous relationship. Again he kept his distance, listening and offering a friendly shoulder to cry on as my relationship with Rene fell apart and again as I met new men in the US. He was happy for me. I became convinced he was the one for me.

The things I felt for the men around me were nothing compared to what I felt for Luis, but he did not seem so sure and maintained that God would take care of each of our need for a partner and that we might or might not be destined for each other. He initially allowed no name for our relationship, and when I asked if he preferred that I defer sex with others until we decided what we could be together, he said that he could not be so egotistical to require anything of me, but simply to wait and see what God had in store. He was completely unselfish and put me first, perhaps saving my life after three unsuccessful relationships where I thought I had found a life partner, but had been disappointed in each near the last minute. I was near depression and near giving up hope, but his friendship and focus sustained me, and my needs to be happy were his primary concerns during my last days in Ecuador and my return to the US. I thank God for Luis. At first, when I tried to move toward a more definite commitment with him, he headed me off for reasons I do not understand, but he still supported me even as I came to know a new American boyfriend who wanted to shut Luis out of the picture. Luis was unselfish in his devotion to me, and that seemed the best way for me to date: to not seek things from others, but to see how I could help them. I got to put that idea quickly into practice as I met a nice man at the grocery store who wanted to be friends but ruled out any enduring relationship with me. He was new to being out and dating, so I sort of became his gay big brother, completing the circle. So second, empathy is a powerful aphrodisiac.

Now three years after my spurt of casual dating, I have left Ecuador and returned again to company headquarters. I think Luis is the man of my dreams and am now marking time until we can finally begin to live together. All we have right now is Truth together. We don't have a daily routine together or ways to tease each other or meaningful looks or an actual sex life together. But we have the truth of our feelings and past experiences with each other as well as our journeys up to this point to keep us together. I still make daily choices that he is the one I want, as I greet him every morning by text, share important news and feelings with him, and I don't seek relationships with others as we wait for the coronavirus crisis to end and he can come and live with me. There are scary moments, as it seems we may have a long wait, but my truth still screams that I want to live my life with Luis. Of course, that truth will not protect us from the virus, and our frustration rollercoaster takes many dives and climbs that we muctdecide how to respond to each. We are choosing to learn a great deal about each other and sharing our truths long distance including how hard this can be and how much we hurt. Tonight I suggested that we find new ways to be intimate by long distance, as I enjoyed looking into his beautiful eyes via video chat. We make choices to suggest action or stay safe in order to show love and wait to be loved. These small decisions are creating our future, so it is important to be in touch with one's truth to make choices in a consistent direction.

Dating Existentialism

I believe I have landed on one nugget of truth in the search for a long-term partner Yes, I want one badly, but I also realized that truth will not make it happen and I had no way of knowing to which man it would eventually lead me. If you are looking for a partner or not, I respectfully ask you to consider this piece of truth for your garden. Our control of a future relationship is in the present, as we choose who to date and spend time and energy on. That's where we have control, and these interactions led me to make decisions about who to interact with tomorrow and the day after tomorrow. Sharing truth and making connections happens now, and while it eventually leads toward the future and has some ability to show which future is most appealing, it does not control the future from today. We need to take each relationship one day at a time without a set road map. In the past, I chose to meet a broad swath of men and not artificially limit them, instead opting for casual dating. For all I knew, I could have become deeply involved with the guy who owns the unfriendly dog. We would have needed to find a way for our dogs to coexist peacefully if we were to ever live together, but that's only one model of a relationship, but I didn't need to worry about methods of dog training at the time I considered asking him out.

I would like to coin a new term, I'll call it existential dating. There is a philosophical term called gay existentialism that hinges on the question of whether homosexuality is a choice (H. Acton, 2010). Since existentialists believe that ethics are established by the choices themselves based on contrast to alternatives rather than being measured by the end result. In the same way, a person looking for a partner is responsible for his or her future relational status almost exclusively based on their day-to-day choices of whom to date and pursue. So there is little sense in worrying about the end goal of a life-long partner on a day-to day basis or to worry if it's about a consistent method, for example, if it's better to talk first or get naked first. My term can be used for any type of dating.

The future partner will arise and become apparent as the shape of a series of choices among and within relationships becomes obvious. Those short-term choices and options will take care of the loneliness the individual sometimes feels, and each date's ability to meet needs for companionship and other truths will influence later decisions about whom to spend time with and what one chooses to do with each, as personal truth and needs will determine how much time the other person wants to spend with you. Neither dating nor truth sharing are about an end goal, but are continuing ends in themselves.

Careful and well-made decisions happen within a relationship too, but either among relationships or within one, individual decisions do not quickly or necessarily lead to eternal bliss, but the decisions move us forward, and choices based on what we value moves us in the direction of our truth. In the end, following my own truth of what I need in life was not easy and took me on a wild adventure in which I learned a great deal about myself and the world around me, no matter how often that world changed. Along with the truth I gained personally, I learned hints toward understanding larger, more universal truth, and even while these larger truths are powerful, it would be wrong of me to impose them on anyone. I learned the importance of discussion with others to attempt to balance our truths together and balance them in relationship, I learned the nature and importance of love, and I see that for me, following my own truth turned out well, although life is not always wonderful.

As I wait for the COVID-19 pandemic to subside to finally live full time with my chosen partner, Luis, I see that life can be tough but that Luis is worth the wait. I have faith that we truly will be a strong couple together, and I sense a real confirmation of my truth that this was the right choice, although the happy ending music is not yet playing. I believe in God and fate and destiny, and I believe that the search for my truth has pointed and guided me to all three.

Appendix 1

Guidelines to Have an Effective Conversation to Share Your Truth

1. Reduce judgment.

   a. Focus your mind and phrasing as statements of self rather than general principle. For example, say "I feel uncomfortable when you do or say XYZ" rather than "XYZ is inappropriate." To state the observation as a general principle implies that anyone one not complying is wrong.

   b. Use *I* statements such as "I feel," "I believe," "In my experience" rather than summaries of perception of the other person such as "You always" or "You treat me like" and encourage your conversation partner to do the same.

2. Have clear goals.

   a. Remember that truth sharing is not blood sport and that there will not be a winner or loser to the event. All participants are intended to be winners with all truths respected.

   b. State your goals out loud and don't be afraid to remind your conversation partner as needed, such as "I want to understand your thinking better" or "I want you to know I respect you a great deal even though I'm choosing a different path."

c. Realize that your emotions may have other sinister goals in mind to beware of, such as "I just want you to shut up and leave me alone." This is not a helpful goal to building relationship, so stating another goal keeps those feelings in their place, and they can have a valid place, but not in those words.

3. Have a stated method in order to proceed effectively. People make jokes about diplomats arguing over the shape and size of the discussion table, but setting the scene and proceeding with purpose do matter.

4.

a. Find commonalities where you can agree in your views. A focus on values will often help reveal commonalities and quickly clarify differences.
b. When you come to differences, affirm the other view as a valid choice, such as "I see the value of consistency."
c. Use the word *and* more than *but*. Find ways to value two ideas at once.
d. Intersperse discussion with opportunities to cool off and take a break. Doing a mutually enjoyable activity during the discussion can provide this escape as needed. Sometimes just calling the discussion to a close is a good move, and be sure to set time to talk again. Some suggestions for activities may be shopping, a sport that leaves enough breath and pauses for discussion such as walking orh iking, batting cages, bowling, or golf.

5. Take care of your conversation partner.

a. Be aware of power positions in the relationship and the activity chosen and balance them to help the less powerful person feel more comfortable. My dad expressed a great deal of care and love for me by choosing to talk through a play with me, an area I am much better at than he is; and in the basic rules of engagement, I became the teacher. This worked as a great counterbalance to the fact that I am the son who traditionally did the listening and that I would have more difficult things to say.

b. Plan your side of the discussion ahead of time for clarity, thinking through possible reactions and difficulties for the other person; but then listen to reactions, concerns, and questions as you deliver the message. It will not go as planned.

c. Actively find ways to offer respect, relief, and affirmation of the other person's views.

d. Think of misunderstanding as the enemy, not your conversation partner or his/her set of beliefs. Relentlessly root out misunderstanding like the noxious weed it is.

e. Actively listen and find ways to show you understand, for example, summarizing what your partner said, asking questions, drawing conclusions of how concepts fit together, and then asking if your conclusion or summary is correct.

f. Ask lots of questions such as "What do you mean by that?" "Why?" or "Does that present a problem when …?" Open-ended questions are often more effective at maintaining a neutral tone than statements or conclusion.

g. Solicit questions. Open-ended questions are often the best, like "How do you feel about that?" is much better than "You have a problem with that?"

h. Paraphrase neutrally and ask for confirmation of what you think you understand, especially if the idea is negative. Avoid accusatory statements such as "Do you mean that you won't allow your child to play with my son anymore if I hold this view differently than you?" Instead, ask "How do you want me to respond to your child when s/he is at my house?"

6. Take care of yourself.

    a. Set boundaries as needed, such as "I can't talk about that anymore right now" or "Please don't refer to XYZ in that way."
    b. Monitor your emotions and clarify those of your partner. Call for a break if feelings start running hot. Confess your feelings about the conversation if needed to cool off or take a change in direction.
    c. Don't be afraid to talk about your intention in a particular statement, word choice, or choice of topic. Unstated or assumed motives can often trigger hot button issues.
    d. If speaking with multiple people at the same time (this often applies to parents), beware of the person who simply agrees with another. Clarify how complete that agreement really is. Also, ask which individuals are included if someone starts to speak for more than just themselves.

Remember that, an individual's comfort with and ultimately the difference between personal truth and absolute Truth is a difference in the belief of the nature of the future. Absolute Truth promises one outcome for all based on an exact recipe as a promise. Personal truth gives no such assurances. It views a world of individuals interacting and connecting with one another in unknown ways. Because of the multiple actors and variables, the outcome in the future is unknown at the start. If someone is insisting on only one correct answer or behavior, it's a good technique to ask why or what may happen if the plan is not followed.

Don't buy the line of people who try to make up universal truths as they go along. In other countries, this was common. For example in Ecuador, a boyfriend who was jealous and physically hit me enough that I fell down and bled came up with the excuse, "That's just how we handle things here." No. Not with me, you don't! That was not OK, not a reasonable excuse.

Appendix 2

Email to My Father, August 25, 2018

The purpose of this e-mail was to explain much of the *why* behind my new attitudes and behavior after coming out, which were troubling him. I offer it here as an example of explaining the self without apology or judgment. It also goes into my psychology in a way that may explain odd bits of me to the reader.

Dad—

I'm going on dates with two different guys this weekend and I sense the day coming fast when I have to decide between them. I'd like to ask for your prayers as I date Rene and Andres. There's a lot in my head and heart about the two, It's really nice to have Juan Carlos to chat with about these guys, and he makes some unique Ecuadorian observations that have shaped my thinking to some degree. Both guys are Ecuadorian. Gretchen [his wife] asked me once not to write about affection between men in order to protect you. This story involves that, so I've given you the headline with my request for prayer. I will now write about the situation and the stories if you want to know more. They're interesting stories, and I'm writing in part to clear my head and to help me sort by talking this out with you. You expressed some interest in my selection process, so here it is raw and wooly. There are also some things I've learned about myself. I will write this starting from the more superficial details to the more intimate. So there are a couple options for you: you can start reading and stop when you've had enough of this kind of thing. No penalty for taking care of yourself and I know you're interested in me, and that's why I'm brave enough to write this frankly. Alternatively, if you feel you need to stop or don't want to go there at all, tell me so, and I'll recreate a PG version of the part or all of it that you didn't want to read. No problem. I want to help you understand me, not shock you or distress you. I'll be frank, by the end, I will probably mention some points about sex, so be warned.

To start with, I'll explain that the male gay guy world divides itself along a scale of how masculine or feminine a man behaves. Separate aspects such as style of dress, attitude, or physical movements may be at different levels along this scale and rated separately. So at one end are very effeminate cross dressers, to guys at the other end who get off on dominating other men. I've seen couples work with all kinds of combinations between the two partners. I've seen two masculine guys work very well together, however, two feminine guys can have a good relationship, but sometimes they can get pretty bitchy with each other. That kind of relationship seems to work better as friends rather than living together, so each gets their own space. I have always been more attracted to masculine guys. I had a relationship with an actual woman, so in this new part of my new life, I don't have much need for feminine beauty. I purposely present myself as more masculine, and that's how I behave in intimate situations as well in pursuing men rather than being pursued. Sometimes guys get a bit confused with me when my arguably more feminine side comes out, including care giving and cooking and being more emotional. I have found myself much more willing to let my emotions show in this new part of my life, maybe because I feel them so strongly. Anyway, the guys I like and successfully date are those who can find and like a balance between us. Expectations can kill a relationship pretty quickly. so there tends to be a period of uncertainty in the beginning as the partners learn about each other and show who they are.

Andres is much more willing and hopeful that I will take the lead in things which puts a certain amount of pressure on me, but overall, I don't mind. I come up with the suggestions for dates and set the pace of our relationship. Juan Carlos pointed out that on his online profile (I met both guys online on the same site) Andres has some very passive wording about relationships, "whether it's for one night or a lifetime . . ." which was a good summary of what I've noticed. I have to be much more direct with him to explain my intentions without scaring him off. Before I take him on the big date today of going to meet people from work, I gave him a list of things that might make him feel uncomfortable about the situation. I don't want him to feel uncomfortable, but I do want to give him the opportunity to opt out or mitigate discomfort if he needs it. If I'm going to lead in this relationship, I want to be able to do so without always looking over my shoulder. I know my life is pretty stressful and pretty socially political, and I hope he's okay with that. I think that's the area where I have the most doubt in my relationship with Andres.

Completely passivity without being able to care for himself will wear me out. I kind of have the opposite problem with Rene. He is charging ahead and setting the pace of our relationship, with my consent. Last night he texted me that he loves me (no man has ever said that to me first) and sent me bunches of virtual roses this morning. It is kind of nice to be pursued. One time at my house, he was very gallant and gave me his hand to lead me. It felt very caring and at the same time very directive. I am not sure how I feel about that sometimes. I like that sort of assertive caring for me and have experienced it before, but presuming that I will follow is not a position that I want to be in, especially given my job and my general approach to life

Rene is still not finished with university, so it's harder to see how he might assert himself as a full adult. He's doing a degree in chemical engineering, so his work prospects in his field are limited, depending on location. I'm seeing him on Sunday, and have asked him to tell me more about what he wants out of life and what his dreams are for the future. I suspect I'm going to need to direct the conversation toward career issues since he seems more sure about relational issues, I suspect he will gravitate toward those.

I feel like there are more unknowns about a relationship with Rene than with Andres, and that does make me feel uneasy. Dating or living with him awhile will not clear up this issue; it's dependent on his graduation and where in the world we might live. The biggest unknown still with Andres is our sex life. Sex is pretty much an unknown in a gay relationship until you get in bed together because of the range of masculine and feminine traits in guys, and their sex style which may or may not correlate. At the conference, I met several Christian gay guys who wanted to take the tradition approach and wait until marriage to have sex. I really don't understand how that would work well, given the range of approaches. Gay guys have a set "bag of tricks" as the Germans put it, but preference for one style or another really depends on each individual and the couple. Whether or not the anatomy actually fits together is also an unknown. Spanish, I think has better words for this difference than English. In English, we call these roles "top" and "bottom" which is a literal picture of anal, penetrative sex. In Spanish they talk about "active" and "passive," which makes sense in so many situations and allows a range and a changing of roles depending on mood and the particular activity. I am typically pretty active, but Andres can be so passive, the whole experience sometimes falls flat for me and I don't feel loved. The cuddling and tenderness are really wonderful with him, and what I need most. After our last encounter, Andres texted me about his plan to be more "active" the next time" maybe he sensed a little disappointment. I think it's funny in the world of texting as part of dating, how guys try to make up for perceived mistakes after a date. I both wish I had and am glad I didn't have that option when I was younger. I would have been a nervous wreck and no action would ever feel complete. It's one thing to cuddle after sex, but a texting afterglow is a bit much to handle.

Anyway, I plan to have (protected) sex with both guys this weekend as well as take each to a big event in public, and time to talk seriously, as well as some time of nothing being planned, and that will mostly sort out my questions about both guys. The thing I don't know is how to end each date. I don't want to declare a winner at the end of any evening. I need time to think and pray and reflect, but we will be intimate enough that both guys will probably want to at least have a plan for the next date, and I'm not ready to give that. For either guy, the next step for me seems to be something like spending Labor Day weekend together. Of course, they don't have that Monday off, but you know which weekend I mean, and that leaves me Monday to myself, which I'm learning to like. Maybe I'll have a clear sense of that by the end of this weekend.

APPENDIX 3

Afterward

After this long and tumultuous search for a life partner, the reader can perhaps imagine how much I wanted to write an ending comment about how wonderful life is with my man, Luis. That would feel really good.

However, life often happens at a different pace and direction than our wishes, and Truth does not change conditions in most cases. My publication deadline is upon me, and the coronavirus still prevents Luis from joining me in the US. Delays are mostly caused by the vagaries of his work; and at the moment, he now has work again, which he loves, and wants to earn more before going again into temporarily uncertain work status as an immigrant. That is his truth that I deeply respect and will actually benefit from. But while my ultimate plan is still unfulfilled, my dream and my truth are intact, and I am already experiencing a deeper love with him than I thought possible. We have a plan to be married in December because that's far enough away to hope virus issues may hopefully have cleared enough to allow for a more traditional and inclusive celebration of our union. Luis also thinks December is especially beautiful and romantic. While we have not been together to officially and grandly propose, he has agreed to let me do so in the future, and we already call each other *esposo* (husband) in Spanish and *osito* (cute bear).

Love continues to grow between us in ways that couples experience in the first months of being together, but we seem to be doing things in a different order. We are finding ways to balance his need to work a great deal (his position has evolved into a telephone representative of an electronics chain) and my need to communicate a great deal. I am good at expressing myself in words, which works well over distance, and he tells me he has never felt so loved or experienced anything as beautiful as I am to him, and he makes time every day to communicate deeply with me and helps me manage my sea of feelings to not feel so alone.

At first, I felt insecure in this type of relationship after being deceived and led along by scammers and liars in my past. But the new beauty of my relationship with Luis is sometimes breathtaking and unexpectedly endearing, like this morning via text, he encouraged me to stay in bed and relax since it's Saturday. Sometimes he imagines my day and makes suggestions of what I can do or what he would like to do with me, and so we live day by day together.

We even have started a sex life together long distance, as we talk about what we want and expect and will enjoy with each other. It feels a little bit like arranging an online hookup, as we chat and exchange sexy pictures with each other, but unlike an online first meeting, the answer is always yes. We have been in each other's embrace previously, and we experience love first, more than anything else.

We both worry and fret at times about the delay and an unknown future, but difficulty seems to burn away the impurities. We see our worries are pointless, as our love and devotion to each other grows daily. We also learn each other's truths as we watch each other struggle and survive. He has read this book, and continues to understand and accept my past and present. We realize the value of each other and every day of life, and I doubt we will have much problem ever taking each other for granted. We see each of our truths grow in strength under the strength and appreciation of the other. Our ideal plan is on hold, but truth, beauty, and relationship continue to grow.

I hope to visit him in Ecuador shortly after their airports reopen to foreign travelers, and he plans to visit here in August when he believes he can take vacation that he is owed. Now almost nine months since I last saw him, my love for him continues to grow in ways I have never seen. I know I am becoming stronger as a person, and my truth continues to blossom despite harsh winds. My truth, that tender plant that sprouted almost five years ago, endures and grows steadily, and that is worth celebrating.

In the loneliness of waiting for the coronavirus to clear, I have also learned another truth about myself. I've faced up to the fact in this narrative that I've become increasingly emotional. However, when nothing felt good and Luis was far away, I discovered my balance between emotion and thinking. Being semi-attached to Luis sometimes did not feel good at all. I did not sacrifice my emotional side, but I realized that I need to balance out some occasionally very strong emotions. There are times when a relationship sucks. When I was a pretending hetero obeying society's whims, I learned how to ignore my feelings and keep going in the direction dictated for me. That meant less emotion and more thinking, but as I have broken free from that prison. I see, too, that emotion cannot always control everything. With Luis far away and little hope of seeing him soon, I sometimes felt hopeless and wanted nothing. Every little annoying thing he did was amplified. I needed to give up on the relationship or unhook myself from emotional decision making to make some thoughtful discoveries: that sex is not magic and that our similar perspective, emphasis on care for each other, and the value to care for each other still unites us, makes us strong, and be a great deal of fun. While I have no hard evidence, these thoughts were enough to create a strong faith in my relationship with Luis that I believe will last many, many years. I hear his voice in my head at difficult moments bidding me to stay calm, which in Spanish and his manner of expression is "calma, calma, calma"

APPENDIX 4

Apologia

While it looks like the word *apology*, this apologia is nothing like an apology. An apologia is an old form of theological writing to give reasons for a belief. It's an argument. While my story has given plenty of examples and anecdotal reasons why I believe and act as I do, a regular drumbeat of believers in an absolute and received truth, who insist on calling me a sinner "because the Bible tells me so," inspired my resolve to include a more direct response about received truth.

My argument here is not that homosexuality is morally acceptable. There are several other authors who have excellently presented this point in better theological form than I can, including David Gushee, Brandon Robertson, and Troy Perry; but instead, I will argue that the development of one's own truth is not in contradiction with the concept of received truth, much as neither science nor religion negate the other.

For the sake of space, I will restrict this apologia to the style and content of Protestant Christian theology because it is the tradition with which I am most familiar. And I wish to apologize to those of other faiths for my current inability to yet fully relate to them as well, and I encourage these believers to expand these ideas into their own traditions.

First, I argue that a literal view of received truth such as biblical text inhibits the intended principles of that tradition and the text.

To begin with, the apostle Paul and several other biblical writers make it clear that being right with God does not come through obeying a list of rules. These rules are often referred to as the Law, which is a reference to the cultural baggage that Jewish Christians brought with them into the new Christian faith: a need to obey all the rules. Sometimes writers use the single issue of circumcision to represent the whole list of rules. The objection to following a list of rules is that it takes the emphasis off what Christians believe to be the source of a human's correct relationship with God and the death and Resurrection of Jesus. Romans 3:19–21 says, "No one will be declared righteous in his [God's] sight by observing the law [following the rules] … But now a righteousness from God, apart from law, has been made known, to which the Law, and the Prophets testify. This righteousness from God comes through faith." This must have been an extremely hot topic in the early Church, as this argument rages through the New Testament that salvation comes through Christ, not obedience to a list of rules. And the side of the argument for following the rules is strangely absent despite that being the preferred practice of many modern Protestants. However, Galatians 5:4 says, "You who are trying to be justified by law have been alienated from Christ; you have fallen away from grace." So to base religious practice on a set of rules in this view is worse than futile; it is counterproductive. Focusing on literal text of what is allowable and preferred behavior is not the way to salvation according to the Bible. In contrast, the argument for following all the rules is a no-show.

Furthermore, the Bible advocates an experiential approach to salvation and knowing God. Psalm 34:8 says, "Taste and see that the Lord is good; blessed is the one who takes refuge in him." It does not say "Study and learn" but encourages us to something deeper than cognitive thought and contemplation. "Taste and see" are sensory, experiential details, and the result will be so positive that the psalmist believes we will take refuge under God's wings, seeking divine protection and salvation. Jesus encourages his disciples to "ask and it shall be given to you; seek and ye shall find" (Matthew 7:7–8). This is encouragement to action and investigation on the part of the individual, not a search for the right scripture reading. The Bible tends to confide in this approach because of a certainty that since the creation of the world, "God's invisible qualities—his eternal power and divine nature—have been clearly seen, being understood from what has been made." In other words, God can be understood by the world around us. Not only should we take caution of falling away from grace by focusing too much on received truth, but there is also an experiential world available through which to understand God. I think Brandon Robertson does a good job of balancing a search for truth in holy texts and through living life in his book *Nomads*. He writes, "While it is true that experience alone is not enough to sustain our lives, it is a major part of what it means to be a human." We should value theology and doctrine as faithful guides along the way, helping us to put language to the indescribable reality that we find ourselves encountering. So there is room, incentive, and fulfillment to be found in pursuing our own truth according to the Bible.

One of my favorite Bible stories that illustrates the balance of received truth with individual truth revelations is the story of Cornelius and Peter in Acts chapter 10. Cornelius was a Roman soldier who the text describes as a "seeker of truth." He had no known religious training except for a likely familiarity with the Roman Pantheon, but he had begun to do good deeds of giving to the poor in Judea, as he questioned and acted upon his concepts of divinity. One day, God suggested that he send for the apostle Peter who was staying not far away. Cornelius did. As I found in my journey, sometimes our personal truth gets a distinct nudge, and while I have no particular point to make about God speaking directly to an individual, I certainly think it's possible. And in my case, external forces pointed me in surprising, new directions, sometimes through no effort of my own, so I am unwilling to take a stand if those experiences are similar or different than being directly addressed by God.

In any case, at the same time, the apostle Peter, who was a strong adherent to his Jewish traditions, experiences his own divine nudge. He was waiting for lunch on a rooftop and fell asleep. He had a dream that a sheet was lowered in front of him and a voice told him to get up, kill, and eat whatever he liked in the middle of feeling hungry. But Peter was a good rule follower and responded that he would rather starve to death because everything in front of him was not kosher. Then he heard the voice of God say, "Let no one call something unclean that I have made clean." This dream repeated a total of three times to make the point extra clear, and about this time, the servants of Cornelius had arrived and were calling out for Peter. Finding him, they invited him to the home of their Roman master. Even entering the home of a non-Jew was also against the rules, but Peter had begun to learn his new truth and agreed to go with the men and actually entered Cornelius's home with no reported fuss. He told Cornelius and his family about Jesus; they became Christians, and Peter's truth expanded to know that God loves and came to save non-Jews as well. This story amazes me because God coordinates two radical and complementary rethinkings of truth, blending the concept of personal and received truth, excluding neither, and making peace between two opposite theological and personal truths. I love God's reported perspective too, "What I have called clean, let no one call unclean." I think that means me, both as a non-Jew and as a gay man. I believe I am clean in God's eyes, and it doesn't matter what anyone else believes about me or a particular set of rules.

Finally, the overall message of Jesus as seen in the Gospels is one of love and inclusion of those less fortunate and on the outskirts of society, while to the rule followers, Jesus said, "You tithe mint, dill, and cumin, and have neglected the weightier matters of the law: justice and mercy and faith!" (Matthew 23:23). Obeying every rule is not the big picture, and it's easy to agree that a focus on the rules can distract us from more important issues as implied here.

God has each of made us unique, with a unique perspective on Truth. I think our own truths are not separate truths, but different perspectives on the big Truth of the universe. We then come closer to the whole as we understand and live our truth, sharing and comparing it with others, accepting their truths as well.

Apendix 5

Hurdles of depersonalization.

As I read over this text, I realized the array of forces set against the individual—sometimes purposely sometimes by tradition or accident—to keep us from our personal truth Here they are in hierarchical order, to look out for:

- Religious scripture or tradition which are expected to trump individual belief
- Someone who "explains this tradition to the individual, often inserting his or her own point of view and makes application for the individual
- Group or societal norms of behavior
- Some individuals who assert their opinion as more important than other individuals'
- Self censorship

There is nothing wrong with these in themselves, but the individual must be careful around them not to lose or experience harm to his or her truth.

INDEX

H

hangouts, gay, 31
homosexuality, 23, 27, 86, 103
hope, 46, 51–53, 70–71

I

"If" (Kipling), 79

J

Jesus, 104
Juan Carlos (friend), 93, 95
judgment, 89, 93

K

Kae (Andrew Phineas's daughter), 21, 39, 58
Kipling, Rudyard, 79
  "If," 79
Köln, 27, 63. *See also* Cologne

L

love, 65, 100
Luis (Andrew Phineas's fiancé), 42, 50, 53–54, 66, 69, 83–84, 87, 99, 101

M

"Major Tom," 29
Matt (friend), 34–36
McGillis, Kelly, 18
Metropolitan Community Churches, 36
Miller, Arthur, 24
  Death of a Salesman, 24

N

norms, 4, 69

O

osito, 99

P

Pantheon, 105
Peter (apostle), 105
petition, 61
Phineas, Andrew
  coming out, 13, 18
  e-mail to his father, 93
  meeting Luis, 54
  with his colleagues, 13–14
  with his dad, 11, 23–25, 90
planning, 15
politics, American, 3
pride, 74
Prodigal Son, 24

Q

questions, open-ended, 91

R

relationships, 15, 23, 35, 46, 53, 79–81, 83
  intimate, 60
  monogamous, 34
  romantic, 60
Rene (Ecuadorian man), 57–58, 60–62, 64, 66, 80, 83
righteousness, 104
rings, 55
Robertson, Brandon, 105

S

salvation, 104
San Francisco, 30
self-care, 68, 70
self-definition, 12, 14, 27
self-disclosure, 9
Spain, 12

statements, *I*, 81, 89
Stergis (friend), 34
Stuttgart, 13, 21, 30, 45, 60, 62–63, 65, 72, 74

T

traditionalists, 8, 49
Truth
    absolute, 2–3, 22, 92
    criteria for one's, 7
    experimental, 38
    identification of, 49

monolithic, 37
nostalgic, 64
personal, 3, 9, 30, 50, 63–66, 68, 75, 82, 92, 105
private, 1, 22, 49, 82
received, 12, 103, 105
sharing, 42, 80–82, 85–86, 89
universal, 83, 86, 92

U

union, 50
uniqueness, 37

CPSIA information can be obtained
at www.ICGtesting.com
Printed in the USA
BVHW080952030820
585324BV00001B/171